On the Nature, Limits, Meaning, and End of Work

READING AUGUSTINE

Series Editor:

Miles Hollingworth

In collaboration with the Wessel-Hollingworth Foundation

Reading Augustine presents books that offer personal, nuanced and oftentimes literary readings of Saint Augustine of Hippo. Each time, the idea is to treat Augustine as a spiritual and intellectual icon of the Western tradition, and to read through him to some or other pressing concern of our current day, or to some enduring issue or theme. In this way, the writers follow the model of Augustine himself, who produced his famous output of words and ideas in active tussle with the world in which he lived. When the series launched, this approach could raise eyebrows, but now that technology and pandemics have brought us into the world and society like never before, and when scholarship is expected to live the same way and responsibly, the series is well-set and thriving.

On the Nature, Limits, Meaning, and End of Work

Zachary Thomas Settle

BLOOMSBURY ACADEMIC
LONDON • NEW YORK • OXFORD • NEW DELHI • SYDNEY

BLOOMSBURY ACADEMIC
Bloomsbury Publishing Plc
50 Bedford Square, London, WC1B 3DP, UK
1385 Broadway, New York, NY 10018, USA
29 Earlsfort Terrace, Dublin 2, Ireland

BLOOMSBURY, BLOOMSBURY ACADEMIC and the Diana logo are
trademarks of Bloomsbury Publishing Plc

First published in Great Britain 2023

Cover design: Terry Woodley
Cover image: Aeronautical Engineers at the Republic Aviation Corporation
Plant at Farmingdale, USA, work on a top secret jet fighter, the Republic F-105.
© Bettmann/Getty

A catalogue record for this book is available from the British Library.

A catalog record for this book is available from the Library of Congress.

ISBN: HB: 978-1-3502-9978-8
PB: 978-1-3502-9977-1
ePDF: 978-1-3502-9979-5
ePUB: 978-1-3502-9980-1

Series: Reading Augustine

Typeset by Deanta Global Publishing Services, Chennai, India
Printed and bound in Great Britain

To find out more about our authors and books visit www.bloomsbury.com and
sign up for our newsletters.

For my parents, Tom and Kim.

*It was you who taught me
how to read,
how to work,
how to put it down,
and how to question everything.*

*I don't expect you will agree with everything here;
what fun would that be?
But I do hope the disagreements are clarifying.*

*And more than anything,
I hope you see something of the fruits
of your labors in these pages,
as they (your labors; not the pages) mean
everything to me
and have pointed me toward that unspeakable more.*

*Is that not, after all, the final meaning and gift of
work?*

CONTENTS

ACKNOWLEDGMENTS

It is still not clear to me how one can or should go about writing a book. I feel as though it's more accurate to say that I revised this text into existence rather than actually having written it. But maybe that is just the nature of my own process. Or of writing in general.

This project began as my dissertation in Vanderbilt's Graduate Department of Religion. The present book's questions and themes are consistent with those of the dissertation, but the structure, language, content, and basic argument have changed significantly. Indeed, it took me proposing, revising, writing, revising again, submitting, and defending an early version of this project in order to gain some level of clarity about everything that then needed to be changed, fixed, nixed, and replaced. In short, I had to write a version of the thing and hear the problems in order to figure out what a sustainable rewrite would entail. I've been circling and re-circling the topic and questions for the last five years.

But I would not have known where to start revising (not to mention where to start nixing) apart from my adviser and dissertation committee's guidance and feedback on the initial draft of this project, different as it is from what will follow. On that front, I owe a special word of thanks to Paul DeHart, who took me on in a time of need. The extent to which I can read critically and write clearly is very much the result of Paul's patient instruction and example (both of which preceded this project's beginning). Readers will never know the amounts of pointless material they do not have to slog through, thanks to his careful editorial suggestions.

Relatedly, the basic contours of this project can be traced back to my first seminar at Vanderbilt with Ellen Armour. In the first week of her Theological Anthropology course (my first at Vanderbilt), I drew on the ungrounded criticisms I had heard for so long and suggested that Augustine was unduly anxious about his embodied status. We rightfully spent the next hour unpacking why this suggestion was so misguided, and I have never been able to un-hear or escape her push toward a more gracious reading of *The City of God* since that memorable class.

I also owe a special word of thanks to Bruce Morrill, whose encouragement and advice throughout this project were both cautionary and energizing. Bruce pushed me when I needed it, warned me of some dangers along the way, and cheered me on the whole time. I will forever remember his simple instructions: "Write about whatever puts a fire in your belly." I often think that my ability to give sustained attention to the questions this text is asking (through revision and revision) was borne of Bruce's simple insights.

Laurel Schneider consistently served as the voice of reason I so desperately needed throughout the process of writing the dissertation. Its very existence and completion are the result of her taking the time to process and challenge, and, in that sense, she contributed as much to the life of the author as she did the actual content of the text. Having to send Laurel whatever I knew she would take issue with proved to be illuminating and clarifying in ways I did not anticipate.

Lastly, I owe a special word of thanks to Steve Long for his feedback during the dissertation stage. Dr. Long's energetic encouragement came when I needed it most, and his feedback has been most welcome.

I was fortunate enough to spend my time at Vanderbilt with a lovely group of colleagues: Jason Smith, Andrew Krinks, Amaryah Armstrong, Hilary Scarsella, Andrew Stone Porter, Kelly Stewart, Rachel Heath, Debbie Brubaker, Htoi San Lu, and Francisco Garcia. Kathryn Tanner said that Christian theology is nothing more and nothing less than a community of unending argumentation regarding the nature of Christian discipleship. I count it all joy to have argued, laughed, complained, and commiserated with that fine group of people during those years. Our weekly gatherings at the Mellow Mushroom on 21st Ave. saw me through, and I hope we prove Tanner right about the unending nature of those tasks.

All of that said, I hope this book reads very different from the dissertation it is developed out of, and my approach to the topic would be quite different apart from my experience in that graduate program. As such, it feels important to name some of the impact those experiences had on the present project to contextualize and frame my own approach.

The questions I began asking about the nature of work, work cultures, productivity, and the association of professional endeavors with one's personal identity were born out of my experience as a graduate student. It was no secret that mine was an overpopulated field. While I was preparing for the potential future work as a college professor, universities were producing more PhDs than ever before while also shifting to short term, adjunct hires. Stable higher-ed employment (as stable as it can be these days) regularly depends on previous teaching experience, quality publications, service, and a progressive research project. So I spent my time in the PhD program piecing together, in my work, as much experience as I could in hopes of creating viable opportunities for future work.

To that end, I was working five different jobs by the end of my time at Vanderbilt, when I began working on this project: I was a graduate student, a teaching and research assistant, a research fellow of a new project program at the university, an editor for a growing journal, and I was teaching three undergraduate classes per semester at two different universities in Nashville (a full-time load for some professors). All of this matters to the extent that the work was (apart from my basic fellowship funding from the university, which was both generous and unsustainable for supporting a life in Nashville, TN) underpaid, short term, contract-based, and supposedly necessary for competitive positioning in future employment searches. My experience as a graduate student in an unstable field provided a clarifying peek into some of the problematic norms of American work culture.

It makes some sense, then, that portions of this project have been presented and published in various arenas. An early version of Chapter 4 was presented in the Augustinian and Augustinianisms Unit at the American Academy of Religion. I'm grateful for the constructive feedback I received from Jonathan Teubner during that exchange. The chapter was first published in *Augustinian Studies* (52.2), and I'm incredibly grateful for the astute feedback of my blind reviewers in that process, as I am for Ian Clausen, who I take to be an editor's editor. Portions of Chapter 5 were first published in *Modern Theology* (37.1), and I'm grateful for Bill Cavanaugh's careful oversight and suggestions in that process. Both publications have permissed my reuse of the materials published there.

In contrast to the fast-paced chaos that was my time in a PhD program, the final stage of this project was carried out during a period of slow transition and discernment, all of which was marked by threads of tenderness, peace, and (relative) stability. While I was teaching history in a public school in Chattanooga, I was undergoing a discernment process for ordination to the priesthood in the Episcopal Diocese of East TN, all of which provided me the freedom to linger with and rethink the contours of what I am proposing here. I'm deeply appreciative for the helpful, clarifying conversations I had in that process with Mtr. Claire Brown, Fr. Joe Woodfin, Fr. Brad Whitaker, Alison Shaw, Heather DeGaetano, Rick Govan, and Greg Miller. I'm particularly grateful for the care of Bishop Brian Cole, who has carved out a space for this kind of work (reading, thinking, writing, conversing) to be a legitimate aspect of ministry in the Church.

Miles Hollingworth has been an ideal editor. I'm certainly grateful for his management of this creative series, but I'm most appreciative of his precise feedback at various stages of my writing process. Miles caught my (admittedly strange) vision for this book from the outset, and he was instrumental in helping me hone and direct it at each stage of development.

I'm also grateful for the many conversations I've been fortunate to have (before, during, and since my time at Vanderbilt) regarding this project with my dear friend Hunter Bragg. He has read many of these pages and taken issue with plenty. And while the project is better because of his time and attention, so am I. The extent to which I find Aristotle's vision of friendship compelling is the result of my experience of having been made better, more open, and more curious by Hunter, whom I miss the absolute hell out of.

It will come as no surprise to those that know me that I am most grateful for Meg Settle. If Rowan Williams is right that an icon is "theology in line and color," then Meg is at once both an icon of the divine mysteries and a proxy of Augustine: she knows me better than I know myself. Even as I write these acknowledgments, Meg, and look back at the last decade of life shared with you, what can be said but that Wendell was right: we're in a forest with a clearing "made in the light for the light to return to." It's often mostly dark, made new each day, and that dark is both richer and more blessed because of the bravery you've exhibited in pressing further into that uncharted territory. Into my uncharted territory. Or, should I say, following Ross Gay, my wilderness? Even still, there remains in me some unspeakable urge to join my wilderness to yours: "thickets, bogs, swamps, and all." I am really just trying to say what he already said his student said: that the process of joining our sorrows, selves, fears, and hopes together is all joy.

Lastly, this book is dedicated to my loving, long-suffering, patient, hilarious, beautiful parents. Thank you for all of your work, which continues shaping and directing my own.

Chattanooga, TN
Lent 2022

A NOTE ON TRANSLATIONS

Wherever possible, I have used translations of Augustine's work from New City Press' *The Works of Saint Augustine: A Translation for the Twenty-First Century*, series editors John Rotelle, O.S.A., and Boniface Ramsey. Unless I indicate otherwise, all Augustine passages and citations refer to this series. A few notable exceptions are *De libero arbitrio*. Translated by Francis E. Tourscher. Philadelphia: The Peter Reilly Company, 1937; *De Opere Monachorum*. 1st pbk. reprint. Fathers of the Church. Washington, D.C.: Catholic University of America Press, 2002; and *De Quantitate Animae*. Translated by Francis E. Tourscher. Philadelphia: The Peter Reilly Company, 1933.

ABBREVIATIONS

c. Prisc.	*Against the Priscillianistis (Contra Priscillianistas)*, tr. Roland J. Teske, S.J. (1995)
conf.	*Confessions (Confessiones)*, tr. Maria Boulding, O.S.B. (2011)
civ. Dei	*The City of God (De Civitate Dei)*, tr. William Babcock (2012)
div. qu.	*On Eighty-Three Varied Questions (De diversas quaestionibus* octoginta tribus), tr. Boniface Ramsey (2008)
doc. Chr.	*On Christian Teaching (De doctrina Christiana)*, tr. Edmund Hill (1996)
en. Ps.	*Expositions of the Psalms (Enarrationes in Psalmos)*, tr. Maria Boulding, OSB (2000–4)
ep.	*Letters (Epistulae)*, tr. Roland Teske, S.J. (1997; 2002)
ep. Jo.	*Homilies on the First Epistle of John (In epistulam Joannis ad Parthos tractatus)* tr. Boniface Ramsey (2008)
Gn. litt.	*On the Literal Interpretation of Genesis (De Genesi ad litteram)*, tr. Edmund Hill (2004)
Gn. litt. Imp.	*On the Literal Interpretation of Genesis, an Unfinished Book (De Genesi ad litteram imperfectus liber)*, tr. Edmund Hill (2004)
Gn. adv. Man.	*On Genesis, against the Manichees (De Genesi adversus Manicheos)*, tr. Edmund Hill (2004)

lib. arb.   *On Free Will* (*De libero arbitrio*), tr. Francis E.
                     Tourscher (1937)

op. mon.   *On the Work of the Monks* (*de opere*
                     monachorum), tr. Sister Mary Sarah
                     Muldowney, R.S.M. (2002)

pecc. mer.   *On the Merits and Forgiveness of Sins and*
                     on Infant Baptism (*De peccatorum meritis*
                     et remissione et de baptism parvulorum), tr.
                     Roland J. Teske (1997)

quant.   *On the Greatness of the Soul* (*De quantitate*
                     animae), tr. Francis E. Tourscher (1933)

s.   *Sermons* (*Sermones*), tr. Edmund Hill (1992)

Trin.   *The Trinity* (*De Trinitate*), tr. Edmund Hill
                     (2012)

Introduction

What's Wrong with Work?

According to economic theory, at least, the last thing a profit-seeking firm is going to do is shell out money to workers they don't really need to employ. Still, somehow, it happens. . . . The answer clearly isn't economic: it's moral and political.

DAVID GRAEBER
"ON THE PHENOMENON OF BULLSHIT JOBS"

Jobs are not big enough for people. It's not just the assembly line worker whose job is too small for his spirit, you know? A job like mine, if you really put your spirit into it, you would sabotage immediately. You don't dare. So you absent your spirit from it.

NORA WATSON, EDITOR
QUOTED IN STUDS TERKEL'S WORKING

The workplace has been changing for some time now. As economist David Weil recently noted in *The Fissured Workplace*, the nature, pressures, and payoffs of work have been drastically changing since the late 1970s, when capital markets dramatically increased pressure on companies to focus on their core competencies alone. This increased pressure led companies to cut costs by shedding nonessential employment. Ceding those nonessential tasks to third-party companies saves money on payroll and benefits alike. Avoiding quality dips (in service and products alike) requires companies to develop (and police) detailed standards for their contract workers, all of which increase the pressure and bureaucratic oversight on workers carrying out these nonessential tasks (Weil 2017, 11–12). Taken together, these factors have created what Weil refers to as the "fissured workplace."

Such fissure certainly pays off for investors, companies, and consumers—hence its pervasiveness. Anthropologist Karen Ho has noted that the drive for profit accumulation is nothing new in capitalism. She notes, "What is clearly unique in the recent history of capitalism in the United States is the complete divorce of what is perceived as the best interests of the corporation from the interests of most employees" (Ho 2009, 3). Operating with a lean core of employees and a flexible network of third-party contract workers often leads to new and improved products sold at lower and lower prices, but those gains come at serious social cost. Drawing on a vast supply of statistical evidence, Weil shows that American workers currently face an increasingly difficult workplace.

Our work-related problems, I believe, are both economic and cultural in nature.

Economic Problems

On the economic front, pensions are falling, huge numbers of low-wage workers lack employer-provided health coverage, and the US Department of Labor continues recovering record amounts of back and stolen wages from employers. For those fortunate enough to have consistent jobs, life consists of labor and recovery. From 2000 to 2012, workplace productivity increased by 23 percent, while real wages increased by less than 1 percent (Ho 2009, 16). According to the Economic Policy Institute, "[s]ince 1979, productivity has risen six times faster than hourly compensation for the typical US worker" ("Job Growth Stays Solid but Wages Disappoint—Again" 2019). The effects of such forms of wage depression are similar to those of unemployment. When laborers are denied benefits and enough hours to make ends meet, taxpayers inevitably pick up the costs of those medical bills and forms of necessary social assistance.

Our labor opportunities and associated incomes are, additionally, intensely gendered and racialized. Women are more likely than men to be counted among the working poor, and Blacks and Latinos alike are more likely to be counted among that group than their white counterparts ("A Profile of the Working Poor, 2018: BLS Reports: US Bureau of Labor Statistics" 2018). Wage disparities correlate to both race and sex, and they traverse nearly every major occupational category the US Bureau of Labor Statistics recognizes ("Labor Force Characteristics by Race and Ethnicity, 2019: BLS Reports: US Bureau of Labor Statistics" 2018). The troubling history of reproductive labor corroborates these trends, highlighting the long history we have of distributing labor according to perceived racial and gender hierarchies.

The difficulty of living on such wages is further compounded when laborers do not receive the full payments contractually owed them, which is shockingly common.[1] Wage theft is a new norm through which some employers discipline and control their labor force. To highlight the magnitude of this problem, the Economic Policy Institute projected the total value of material property stolen in the States in 2012 to be $340 million. The amount recovered from wage theft (i.e., not the total amount stolen) in the same time period was $933 million (Meixell and Eisenbrey 2014).

Cultural Problems

The problematic nature of the fissured workplace raises interesting questions regarding our cultural assumptions about our work as well as our relationships to our work. In February 2019, Derek Thompson wrote about our uniquely American, obsessive relationship to work for *The Atlantic* (Thompson 2019). Thompson begins by noting that famed economist John Maynard Keynes, in 1930, predicted that America would settle into a fifteen-hour workweek by the turn of the twenty-first century (Keynes 2012; Thompson 2019). Given the rise of automation and automated technology, one has to

---

[1]This analysis is clearly most concerned with wage-based employees, but I am convinced many of the problematic dynamics undergirding the plight of laborers also animate the labor and economic lives of business owners, stockholders, and various levels of management as well. The problems of contemporary capitalism are not uniquely confined to the experience of low-level employees.

wonder both why Keynes' prediction did not materialize and why the American workforce works so much more (and so much more obsessively) than other developed countries. Thompson argues that "workism" is the only coherent explanation—"the belief that work is not only necessary to economic production, but also the centerpiece of one's identity and life's purpose; and the belief that any policy to promote human welfare must *always* encourage more work" (Thompson 2019, 1.2). And Thompson has some compelling data to support the claim. For instance, the US averages more hours worked per year than any other large country with comparable levels of production. We work more, take fewer vacations, retire later, and we do so while receiving less unemployment, disability, and retirement benefits than comparably rich nations. This is particularly astounding given the absurd work hours that rich men—those statistically most able to work the least—log on a weekly basis. Perhaps, then, as David Graeber's epigraph suggests, the drive for work is more emotional, cultural, or spiritual than it is economic.

We inhabit a culture that insists that our life's meaning is bound up in our work, we experience constant pressures at work to be more efficient and productive, and we know the ways in which our work structures contribute to a seemingly ever-growing, corrosive system of poverty and oppression. Studies show that the majority of Americans hate their work, and yet we continue working at dangerous rates given our deeply engrained work ethics. These cultural assumptions regarding work, along with a cluster of other labor-related problems (i.e., automation, wage depression, wage theft, the rise of a flexible labor force, a lack of worker representation, overwork, and productivism) have rightfully cued us to begin asking questions about the nature and meaning of our work, only to discover how much we hate what we do.

The paradox of our insistence on working so much is that an alarming amount of working people hate their jobs. Gallup recently estimated that some 87 percent of employees are not "engaged" at work (Thompson 2019, 1.4). As anthropologist David Graeber noted in his *Bullshit Jobs*, recent polling revealed that "in the United Kingdom only 50 percent of those who had full-time jobs were entirely sure their job made any sort of meaningful contribution to the world, and 37 percent were quite sure it did not" (Graeber 2019, 6). Perhaps even more confounding is the fact that these "bullshit jobs"—which Graeber defines as "a form of paid employment that is so completely pointless, unnecessary, or pernicious that even the employee cannot justify its existence even though, as part of the conditions of the employment, the employee feels obliged to pretend that this is not the case"—tend to offer good working conditions and pay (Graeber 2019, 9–10; 14).

We tend to believe one's meaning is largely discoverable in and through one's work. But Thompson wisely notes that such a broad, if thin, cultural sentiment is a recipe for disaster. What form of self-actualization do we expect to see in a struggling cashier or unhappy barista forced to stay in their jobs by their economic precarity alone?[2] Perhaps the only thing more common than major news outlets insisting that millennials care more about meaning than income is an over-worked millennial experiencing severe anxiety and depression (Bertino 2017; Moore 2014; Vesty 2016; Thompson 2019, 2.6). As Thompson notes, "There is something slyly dystopian about an economic system that has convinced the most indebted generation in American history to put purpose over paycheck" (Thompson 2019, 2.8). It is no real surprise, then, that this approach to work has created a culture of burnout and exhaustion (Griffith 2019).

This matters in that even if one can wash their hands of the structural inequalities stemming from everyday work, overcome the uphill battle of wage discrimination, and survive in a period marked by rising trends of wage theft, they are still likely to have to reckon with the simple insight that, more often than not, work makes us miserable (Hardoon 2017; Cooper and Kroeger 2017). We inhabit a culture that insists that our life's meaning is bound up in our work, we experience constant pressures at work to be more efficient and productive, and we know the ways in which our work structures contribute to a seemingly ever-growing, corrosive

---

[2]These two examples are not aimed at denigrating that class of individuals genuinely interested in working as cashiers or baristas. Rather, I am trying to point to the unfortunate lot who have no interest in their professional roles. These are those workers who were forced to take their job due to their economic precarity, be that immanent bill due-dates or a lack of qualification and opportunity for other more interesting roles. That is, my primary problem is with the cultural pressure to flourish within such a "vocation," even when so many have so little interest in the hourly wage jobs they are currently working.

system of poverty. We hate this work, and yet we continue working at dangerous rates.

We experience myriad injustices and disappointments in work, yet we rarely ask questions about its nature, meaning, or limits.

An Augustinian Proposal

Perhaps surprisingly, St. Augustine offers us—in piecemeal fashion—elements with which we can assemble an alternative vision. With his theology of creation and biblical commentaries, we can develop a theory of the nature of work in the garden, which helps to position that particular mode of agency in relation to the human's end. Through his theology of sin we can articulate the negative effects of disordered love on our various forms of agency and working lives. By examining his understanding of the role of work in the context of the monastery, we see his understanding of both the ways we should undertake our work and the ends toward which we should direct that work during our lives in a sinful world. And in his analysis of the competing visions of agency represented by Mary and Martha in Luke 10, we learn of his understanding of the eventual displacement of work by *sapientia* in the eschaton, which has a great deal to tell us about how we ought to work while we wait in hope of such a future.

The basic task of this book is to draw on these piecemeal treatments of work scattered throughout St. Augustine's varied writings in order to develop and articulate a unified theology of work. More particularly, it is to sketch an Augustinian treatment of the nature, limits, meaning, and end of work. In so doing, this project will push Augustinian studies toward a more detailed engagement with issues of political economy—an area the author believes to be drastically under-explored in the recent resurgence and appropriation of Augustine's thought. This project is premised on the insight that St. Augustine offers us a profound set of resources through which we can develop a distinct understanding of the nature, limits, meaning, and end of work through which we can reshape our working lives and selves.

Given the ways our economy overemphasizes and exploits our working capacities and identities, work offers us unique opportunities for either disintegration or prayerful formation into the life of God. In light of that context, the basic thesis of this book (which I take to be Augustinian in nature), is that work is a uniquely human phenomenon which must be endured, properly related to, and thereby directed toward the love of God, even as we await (in hope) that day when contemplation of God displaces and abolishes productive agency altogether.

Such a project is significant for the field of Augustinian studies, I believe, for three reasons. First is that body of scholarship's void of rich analysis of political economy. I have found, in both Augustine and political Augustinianism, a helpful way of thinking about faithful Christian engagement with contemporary political structures (Mathewes 2008, 2010; Gregory 2010; Bretherton 2009; Dodaro 2008; Griffiths 2012; O. O'Donovan 2003; Williams 2016e). These thinkers recognize in Augustine a way to name the unjust, ideological, and idolatrous shortcomings of both structures and individual practices. At the same time, they use Augustine to strike a balanced vision that avoids what I take to be three generally unhelpful ways of articulating Christian political life: (1) abstracted retreat wherein one altogether fails to articulate the political implications of the Christian faith; (2) the unrealistic attempt to posit and develop a uniquely Christian, isolated political system or practice; and (3) the utopic tendencies of much contemporary, progressive theological discourse. Political Augustinianism—and Augustine himself, for that matter—offers a more realistic, difficult path through which those hoping to be counted among the city of God must travel, and I find that to be very exciting indeed.

To date, however, little work has thoroughly examined the resources in Augustine's theological system for questions of contemporary economic life. As a result, scholarship regularly endorses a vision for political life devoid of any notion of political economy (W. Brown 2017; Sandel 2012; Bauman 2000; Cohen 2003). Without an adequate analysis of the crucial role that capitalism plays in structuring contemporary politics and American life, we severely misrepresent the nuanced mechanics, pressures, and needs for structuring a faithfully Christian sketch of public life.

This project is an attempt to begin remedying that gap by extending the recent work of political Augustinianism into the economic sphere by developing an Augustinian theology of work.

The second reason, while clearly being related to the first, is much more particular in nature: work is an under-analyzed theme in Augustine's writing. To the extent that this project is successful, it should also reveal and characterize a thread running throughout the whole of Augustine's theological works, cutting a new cross-section through Augustine's thought from top to bottom. Augustine speaks of work in myriad ways, and the topic(s) appear throughout the entirety of his oeuvre. This project attempts to trace that thread and systematize its insights so as to make plain the wealth of Augustine's thoughts on the topic.

Third, this project represents a new way of connecting the early and late Augustine, and it does so by bypassing continuity rhetoric. The benefit of such an approach is that it analyzes a topic consistently treated in Augustine's work from as early as 388 (via *De Quantitate Animae*) to as late as 427 (with the completion of *De Trinitate*). Given the consistency through which Augustine treats the topic, this project will connect Augustine's earliest works to his latest without getting lost in the weeds of the continuity/discontinuity debates.

The Argument

To think with Augustine about work requires that we first say something regarding the sort of thing a human being is and the ends for which it was created. Work's nature and meaning are only legible in relation to the human being's purpose, nature, and place within the order of creation. Drawing on *De Trinitate* and *De Quantitate Animae*, the task of this first chapter is to situate work in relation to the final end of the human—knowing and loving God—in and through an exploration of the capacities of the soul. For Augustine, there is no coherent vision of the self totally distinct from God. The soul is crucially bound up in the self's pursuit of God precisely because the mind is said to be the rational capacity of the soul. The soul is the image of God in that it makes possible the human's search for and proximity to God, but it also structures the basic perpetuation and experience of creaturely life in general (i.e., animation, sensation, discursive reasoning, *virtus*, *tranquilitas*, *ingressio*, and *contemplatio*). When read in this regard, work can be understood as any creature's rationally understood, productive agency, which depends on a range of the soul's capacities. Our animal life necessitates some form of work, and our economies and cultures have commodified and economized that work since the agricultural revolution. Amid these swirling pressures and demands, Augustine nonetheless insists that the activity itself be directed toward the human's final end—God. This is the ethical task of work.

In Chapter 2, I argue, with Augustine, that labor's value and dignity stem from creation. In the creation narratives, humans find a certain obligation to labor. That is, the injunction to labor did not stem from the fall. Rather, Augustine reminds his readers that humanity labored in the garden prior to the fall, even if that labor was qualitatively different than what laborers experience today. Labor was no hardship in the garden; it was more akin to a spontaneous experience of joy grounded in creaturely agency. As Augustine notes in *De Genesi ad litteram*,

> The things created by God grew more exuberantly and fruitfully through the concurrent work of man, resulting in more copious praise of the Creator himself who had given to a soul consigned to an animal body the intellect and faculty of rational activity in proportion to the willingness of the spirit, and not in proportion to the necessity of satisfying the needs of the body. (*Gn. lit.* VIII.8)

Beginning with the nature of work in the garden tells us something important about both the confluence of agencies that make humans' work possible and the role that work is to play in the life of the person before God.

It is only after the fall that labor became difficult under divine curse. Chapter 3 examines both the effects of sin on work and the nuanced moral challenges of working under the condition of sin. The difficulty of work under divine curse is due, Augustine explains, to the transformation of the will in the fall. The fall effects work in and through "rendering created realities perishable (or 'contingent')" (Kidwell 2013, 779). As is the case for so many of the topics Augustine treats, the problem(s) with work is more about us than the work itself. That is, the problem(s) tends to stem from the ways in which humans sinfully work or engage with work as sinners in a sinful world. But because Augustine wants to navigate the sinful world faithfully, thinking with Augustine about the effects of sin on work also requires that we consider the possibilities for faithful work, particularly when our world so regularly fosters unhealthy attachments to our work, working identities, and the fruits of our labors. Augustine's use/enjoyment framework, I am arguing here, has profound implications for the ways we undertake our work amid such a context. Much like we are to use our neighbors for the enjoyment of God, thereby loving them properly and humanly, so too are we to "use" ourselves toward that gracious end in work. As Augustine notes, we "are ourselves also things" (*doc. Chr.* I.20). He thinks this is implied in Jesus' commandment to love our neighbor as ourselves. As such, we must use ourselves "for the sake of the one whom we are to enjoy." Every aspect of our persons—all agency, projects, and professional undertakings—"must be whisked along toward that point to which the whole impetus of [our] love is hastening." The self—and its work —can only be properly used, loved, and related to when placed in service of one's enjoyment of God. The task, then, is learning how to properly "use" and thereby love ourselves in order to direct our labor in service of others and our higher callings. The ethical standard is clear enough, but the mechanics by which that standard is met must be sketched next.

The good news is that Augustine offers us some concrete examples of the ways in which we can properly use ourselves for the enjoyment of God. Even within a sinful world, Augustine insisted throughout his theological oeuvre that labor has both dignity and value. Augustine manages to affirm the dignity of labor without universalizing it, mandating it, or even denigrating life outside of labor time. One's moral duty to labor, Augustine argues (along with the vast majority of the class of Roman cultural elites to which he belonged) is actually a subset of one's broader civic duties, and it is a necessary component of the social fabric in our fallen world. From within such a framework, the moral and spiritual task of faithful work is to properly use oneself for the sake of enjoying God, which necessarily entails properly loving my self, my limits, my God, and my neighbor in and through my working experience. Such possibilities are best demonstrated in Augustine's short text *de opere monachorum*, through which he addressed a particular, local issue of monastic discipline and theology involving a labor strike. After briefly overviewing the text and its most relevant insights (for the topic at hand), I argue in Chapter 4 that labor can play a crucial role in one's temporal progression toward the beatific vision when it is properly related to, directed, undertaken, and contextualized. This is true in spite of the emphatically noncentral role labor plays in Augustine's theological anthropology (not to mention the cursed nature of such modes of agency during our lives in the world). The context and manner in which labor is undertaken and carried out, it turns out, makes all the difference, and that difference is only ever actualized through the transformative power of grace. When undertaken in this manner, labor becomes but one element of a larger life of liturgy and prayer. Similar to Pierre Hadot's distinction between philosophical discourse and the philosophical life—a series of existential commitments that structured the entirety of one's being in the world, of which philosophical discourse was a crucial but singular part—the context of the labor situates the activity within a larger form of being or way of living. Under such conditions, I argue, it is possible for labor to become a modality of prayer.

In the fifth and final chapter, I develop a constructive, Augustinian treatment of the end of work. I draw on Augustine's reading of Mary and Martha's competing agencies in Luke 10 to characterize work as a distinctly human, sinful phenomenon that must be endured during our lives in the world, even as we hope for its eventual abolition in the eschaton. Such an approach relativizes economic value and contests our overestimation and valuation of productive agency in the economic sphere. More particularly, it spells out some practicalities for navigating contemporary economic life that avoid both escapism and any overestimation of economic agency or justice.

A Few Final Caveats: On How I Read Augustine and What I'm Not Saying

Augustine is, to be sure, an overburdened character. Given the massive amount of literature that posits drastically opposing views regarding Augustine's theological-political ethics and the historical and cultural distance between the North African bishop and myself, I am under no impression that I have "gotten Augustine right," as it were. Following Charles Mathewes strategy of thinking with the Augustinian tradition, I aim to follow a different path: "I mean to draw guidance from Augustine's thought, without being trapped in the historical cul-de-sac of debates about what Augustine 'really meant'" (Mathewes 2008, 19). I have certainly labored to read Augustine with care and to take him at his word as best I can, but I am far more interested in a particular appropriation of Augustine toward theological engagement of economic issues than qualms of interpretation in Augustinian studies alone.

As such, this project undertakes what Peter Ochs refers to as "depth historiography": developing a set of claims faithful to the plain sense of an ancient text that also aims to deploy those insights toward an issue of urgency in the reader's own context (Ochs 2011, 2002). Undertaken in this manner, the task is less about making Augustine speak to the demands of contemporary capitalism than it is drawing on resources in Augustine's oeuvre with which to think about how one ought to work within the context of contemporary capitalism. I am, to be sure, trying to think with Augustine about work from a dramatically different context and economy, but I have found valuable resources in that North African bishop's writings with which to navigate my own world.

When undertaken in this manner, my attempt to make use of Augustine's theological system for contemporary economic questions neither assumes nor implies any continuity between late antique Roman economies and contemporary capitalism. My strategy here does not depend on articulating any analogy between these two vastly different economies and modes of economic thought. I am simply suggesting that some of the theological and ethical principles salvageable from Augustine's analysis of the commonwealth (which I will eventually demonstrate contains certain economic elements) can and should inform our own relationship to the ways in which we collectively produce, distribute, and use wealth in contemporary society. I am therefore trying to articulate the economic implications of a certain theological ethic operative in a host of Augustine's texts. The labor structures operative in the Roman Empire are, to be sure, vastly different than those that are operative in contemporary capitalism, but such a historical gap need not preclude either an appropriation of Augustine's theorization of the nature of productive activity or the theological implications of properly relating to one's work.

That being said, the task of this project is to read Augustine as an icon through which we can come to see ourselves, our agencies and labors, and our final ends in new light.

1

Being a Creature That Works

If we want to challenge the idea that theology and economics do belong in completely separate frames, the first thing we need to do, paradoxically, is to hang on to the idea that there really are different ways of talking about human activity and that not everything reduces to one sovereign model or standard or value.

ROWAN WILLIAMS
"THEOLOGY AND ECONOMICS"

We need to understand in what sense it is said both that man is made in the image of God and that man is earth and is going to go to earth. The first statement refers to the rational soul, which God bestowed on man—that is, on his body—by creating on him or, if the term is more apt, by inspiration. The second refers to the body, which God fashioned from dust and to which the soul was given so that it might become an animal body—that is, so that the man might become a living soul.

AUGUSTINE
DCD XIII.24

Introduction

To think with Augustine about work requires that we first say something regarding the sort of thing a human being is and the ends for which it was created. This is because when examined in an Augustinian register, work's nature and meaning are only legible when read in relation to the human being's purpose, nature, and place within the order of creation.

Drawing on *De Trinitate* and *De Quantitate Animae*, the task of this first chapter is to situate work in relation to the final end of the human—knowing and loving God—in and through an exploration of the capacities of the soul.

In order to connect work with that final end, I begin this chapter with an extended analysis of one of Augustine's most frequent metaphors for the life of the Christian: work. I analyze that metaphor at length in order to highlight the spiritual connotations of the term. Work's meaning is certainly not solely bound up in the spiritual insights the metaphor makes available, but the metaphor does structure and direct Augustine's understanding of the meaning and purpose of work. Unpacking the metaphor's layers also enables me to sketch some of the most crucial elements of Augustine's anthropology. That is, the metaphor's logic depends on a certain rendering of the human as well as the final ends for which the human was created. And so exploring the metaphor of work thereby enables my exploration of the nature and purpose of the activity in question. In the end, the metaphor of work will reveal something crucial about the physical act of work—its meaning is only legible in relation to the final end for which humans were created.

After exploring the metaphor, I briefly sketch some of the key, foundational points of Augustine's theological anthropology. This excursus allows me to highlight Augustine's understanding of the final end and purpose of human being (i.e., knowing and loving God) so as to situate work within the larger context of life. Because for Augustine there is no coherent vision of the self (or its agency) that is totally distinct from God, understanding the nature and meaning of work requires we first understand the nature and meaning of the human that does that work. Doing so, Augustine insists again and again, requires coming to know the God that is both the creator and end of that human.

Because the soul is crucially bound up in the self's pursuit of God, I then briefly canvas Augustine's understanding of the soul. I do this to situate work within the larger nature and end of the human. For Augustine, the soul enables a wide range of activities: everything from sensation and movement to rational understanding and contemplation of God (in humans, at least). That is, all living creatures have souls that animate their being, but those souls range in complexity and capacity. All living things, for example, have souls capable of animation and sensation, while only humans have souls capable of rational perception. As I will demonstrate, work depends on a diverse range of the soul's capacities. The basic functions are made possible by the lower levels of the soul (i.e., animation and sensation), but analyzing and understanding that work (in order to properly relate to it) depends on the higher functions of the soul.

This is precisely why I define work as any rationally understood productive activity. Because discursive reasoning is only operative in the human, perceiving that agency (and therefore carrying out work) is a uniquely human phenomenon. When read in this regard, our animal life necessitates some form of work, and our economies and cultures have commodified and economized that work since the agricultural revolution. Amid these swirling pressures and demands, Augustine nonetheless insists that the activity itself be directed toward the human's final end—God.

If this chapter is successful, it should accomplish the following, in turn: (1) overview Augustine's metaphorical treatment of sanctification and moral formation in terms of work; (2) articulate the ways his entire theology of work can be seen in his use of this metaphor; (3) communicate the basic building blocks of Augustine's theological anthropology; (4) survey his theory of the soul; (5) frame work as a particular function of the soul; and (6) clarify the ways in which this particular function of the soul should related to the human's final end (i.e., knowing and loving God) by way of the soul.

Work as Metaphor

Sometime around the year 500, Augustine wrote two letters to a layman named Januarius in order to answer his questions about differing religious practices and calendars. While Augustine recognized these long texts as discrete books in his *Revisions*, they are typically treated as standard modes of epistolary exchange (*ep.* 54). The second of these letters is a helpful example of Augustine's usage of "work" as a metaphor for sanctification. In it we see how Augustine utilized work and rest as metaphors in his theological and pastoral writings. He regularly phrases our eschatological encounter with God in terms of rest and our struggle to conform ourselves to Christ during our lives in the world in terms of toilsome labor.

In answering Januarius' question about why Christmas is not celebrated as a sacrament, Augustine ends up writing about the Christian's movement from death to life. While we have passed from death to life in baptism, our resurrection is yet to come (*ep.* 55.4–5). According to Augustine, we remain in the Pauline "now and not yet." He writes:

> This renovation of our life, therefore, is indeed a passage from death to life that first takes place through faith in order that we may rejoice in hope and may be patient in tribulation as long as our exterior self is still being corrupted, but our interior self is renewed from day to day [see 2 Cor 4:16]. On account of the very beginning of a new life, on account of the new self that we are commanded to put on, while we take off the old self [see Col 3:9–10], we throw out the old year in order that we may be new dough, for Christ, our Pasch, has been immolated [see 1 Cor 5:7]. (*ep.* 55.5)

Within this schema, the final end for which the human is aiming—final union God in the end—is characterized as a form of rest. That rest, Augustine believes, stems from our proximity to God, who is the abundant, loving source of all goodness and existing things. If by the term "heaven" we mean that time-space wherein we see God face to face, then heaven will be characterized by rest precisely because we (by way of God's abundant self) will lack for nothing. Augustine writes,

> For we are now, as I said above, living in exile in faith and hope, and what we are striving to attain by love is a certain holy and perpetual rest from all the toil of all our troubles. . . . In that rest, however, there is not a lazy idleness, but a certain ineffable

tranquility of leisurely action. After all, we shall in the end rest from the works of this life so that we rejoice in the action if the next life. (*ep. 55.*17)

He goes on to clarify that this is not a mode of productive activity that corresponds to the work we know during our lives in the world; it is, rather, a kind of perpetual rest in praising God, even if that rest entails a form of action (i.e., praise). And this is why the Sabbath represents, trains us in, and prepares us for that eternal rest that can only be found in God (*ep. 55.*17).

Hoping in that restful end, Augustine believes, should transform the way we experience toil while we are in the world. We are to toil faithfully, patiently now in hope of the coming rest. This metaphor (i.e., the growth of the life of the Christian as a kind of work), highlighting toil and struggle as it does, tells us a few key things about Augustine's understanding of our time during the world.

According to Augustine, the Holy Spirit provides Christians with the motive and power to throw off the chains of sinful delight and begin accepting the saving truth of Jesus Christ. Following one of his favorite passages of Scripture—Romans 7—Augustine recognizes that Christians in this phase, as Mark Clavier helpfully explains, are stuck between two masterful, persuasive orators pulling them in opposite directions (Clavier 2018, 75). Being under grace does not mean the end of sinful desires and impulses, but it does mean that Christians have been given, through the Holy Spirit and the gift of grace, the means to choose better ends. And the tasks of the Christian, which Augustine believes are helpfully characterized in terms of "work," are to regularly resist sin, put on virtue, and thereby conform oneself to the goodness that is the Good itself (i.e., Jesus Christ) in the mundanity, sorrow, and beauty of everyday life.

It is the conceptualization of sanctification in terms of work that is most interesting to me here. The task is to put the old self to death and take on Christ in order to prepare for that final rest. This is why it makes sense for Augustine to write that our struggles to put on virtue "are, of course, also good works, but they are, nonetheless, still full of toil, though their reward is rest. But Scripture says, *Rejoicing in hope* (Rom. 12:12), in order that, when we think of our future rest, we may work at our labor with joy" (Augustine 2002b, II/2:55.25). Our growth into God is itself a kind of work made possible by grace; putting on Christ is toilsome given the ways we have chained ourselves to sinful habits, but we are to undertake that work in hope of the rest that is to come (*ep. 55.26*). These are good works, full of toil, aimed at rest.

Beginning with the metaphor of work helpfully orients my investigation of the nature, meaning, and end of the literal act of working because the metaphor strangely bears the most basic elements of an Augustinian theology of work: the way we currently experience work is the result of sin (and therefore quite different than whatever counted as work in Eden); we have been given the grace to choose better ends and faithfully navigate a fallen world, even now; work will be eschatologically abolished; and hoping in that end should transform the way in which we undertake that toilsome activity during our lives in the world. Put simply, we are to work now in light of the end toward which we are headed: being in God.

But in order to determine how we are to undertake our work in light of the end toward which we are headed, we must first get clear on the nature of work. And to think about the nature of work with Augustine requires we spend some time thinking through the nature of the one who works. It is to this question of the human and the nature of work I now turn.

Augustine's Anthropology: A Briefing

Being Oriented toward God

From the beginning of the first book of *The Confessions*, Augustine sketches a self whose beginning is not grounded in itself. Our only hope for coherency, he tells us, depends on seeing the beginning of our lives in God, as begun by God. It is, in fact, in trying to be our own beginnings that sin emerges (Mathewes 2003, 9). Augustine begins his textual presentation of himself by pointing to an altogether different text (Psalms), a different voice (David), and by reflecting on a subject distinctly not himself (God) (*conf.* I.1.1.; Mathewes 2003, 10). In trying to make sense of the question of himself, Augustine finds the mystery of God to be the hermeneutic key. That is, for each topic Augustine takes up in his attempt to narrate his own creaturely life, he gives God ultimate priority in that the meaning of any given topic only becomes legible in relation to God as creator. God exists before the world (and outside of time, for that matter) begins. God is beyond and prior to space as well; in fact, God's being creates the conditions for spatiality and distinct objects to be at all (Mathewes 2003, 11). Perhaps it is not as strange as one might imagine, then, that the most detailed and programmatic anthropological vision Augustine gives us comes in a book on *The Trinity* and that so much of his "auto-biography" necessarily veers into mystical reflections on the nature of God we love but do not know much of (Mathewes 2003, 10).

All of this matters to Augustine (and for our project of identifying the place of work in his theological anthropology) because the first thing we can and should say about ourselves is, in fact, not about ourselves at all. Rather, we should begin with words of thanksgiving to the gratuitous source of our being. We are only, and always, secondary effects of God's gracious love. In coming to terms with our true beginning, he has already begun to show us our true ends— gratuitous praise and love of the one who gives us life (Mathewes 2003, 11). Augustine writes, "By continence the scattered elements of the self are collected and brought back into the unity from which we have slide away into dispersion" (*conf.* X.29.40). Our lives and actions are therefore reducible to response (i.e., confession) (Mathewes 2003, 11). And the proper response of a creature before its creator, Augustine will insist, is proper enjoyment—worship. Augustine writes, "Let me not waver from my course before you have gathered all that I am, my whole disintegrated and deformed self, into that dearly loved mother's peace, where are lodged the first-fruits of my spirit, and whenever I draw my present certainty, so that you may reshape me to new form, new firmness, for eternity, O my God, my mercy" (*conf.* XII.16.23). Whatever experience we might have of being a self, Augustine insists that it is properly oriented toward a mode of becoming before God in worship.

For Augustine, this basic pattern is not exclusively true for the human—ontology's very structure is patterned around God's triune nature. He infamously argues that various trinities structure both the world at large (*modus, species/forma, ordo*) and humanity's self-conception (memory, understanding, will), and each of those trinities are themselves somehow patterned after God's triune nature. Hence to know or be or do is always to rely on God for the very condition of such an act. The recognition of that pattern, Augustine thinks, does not slip into any overly determined doctrine of God that might violate God's transcendence. Our minds are unable to properly grasp or name God precisely because God transcends created categories. The categories might speak some sliver of truth regarding God, but God continually overflows them; God exceeds their borders and cannot be rendered therein (Mathewes 2003, 12). God simply cannot be possessed in this way, and the struggle to possess in this manner is itself a corrosive, misdirected love that only further perpetuates one's alienation from God (Williams 2016a, 9). Augustine argues that it is this feature of transcendence—the exceeding of every attempt to name or determine whatever it is that God, as the ground of being and order, is—that serves as the spark for this self-conscious reflection (Mathewes 2003, 13). He finds a generative line of inquiry in our failure to know God and our failure to speak of ourselves coherently apart from God. Again, from the outset of *The Confessions*, he is more interested in being grasped by God than grasping God: "What I now longed for was not greater certainty about you, but a more steadfast abiding in you" (*conf.* VIII.1.1). The attempt at understanding takes the form of a request to the God who is the source and ground of knowledge: "Grant me to know and understand, Lord" (*conf.* I.1.1; Mathewes 2003, 13).

This is a selfhood grounded in spectatorship rather than self-awareness or presence. The goal is to come to see one's place in the larger narrative of salvation so as to play one's part in the larger chorus and to find one's voice in the script of things (Mathewes 2003, 13). Hence the anti-autobiographical nature of *The Confessions*. Because auto-biography is self-orienting, it is ultimately limiting in that it misunderstands our experience and ontological structure. Augustine is, at least partially, aiming to make that sort of straightforward, narratival presentation of one's self unintelligible. To whatever extent we have the potential for a coherent understanding of ourselves, it must come through some other's action, that is, God's governance of the created order and some future time we are not yet privy to (Mathewes 2003, 22). As Mathewes crucially notes, by the end of the first book of *The Confessions*, we are faced with the destabilizing insight that whatever potential we have for understanding ourselves rests in coming to terms with our own incomprehensibility. This is a knowing in unknowing, and it forces a certain openness to that which is outside of us. This God who is external to us, who serves as the very ground and end of our being, is not the sort of thing we can force our wills upon. In this orientation toward God, we must learn to accept what will be, to receive our being, potential, and meaning as a gift from the God to whom we are ultimately oriented (Mathewes 2003, 22).

Dialogical Selfhood

The very framework of *The Confessions* reads as a testament to the necessarily logical connections between the experience of finite being and an altogether gracious, gratuitous, and infinite creator (Williams 2016a, 4). Within that framework, Augustine insists that in order to establish what and who I am, I must be in conversation with the God giving me being and calling me to itself. This is why, after all, *The Confessions* is a prayer: "I know myself less clearly than I know you. I beg you to reveal myself to me as well, O my God, so that I may confess the wounded condition I diagnose in myself to my brethren, who will pray for me" (*conf.* X.37.62).

There is, to be sure, a plurality of meanings at work in Augustine's use of the term "confession": acknowledgment, pronouncement of thanks, admission of fault, praise, and so on (Williams 2016a, 3). The process of coming to know myself depends on each of these varied acts of confession, which means that speaking coherently about any one aspect of myself requires I also learn to speak about the God who is both the ground and end of the creature. The grammatical structure of the language we use to make sense of the various aspects of our lives (self, world, other) ends up having God at its center. God serves as the anchor and ground of the possibility of saying anything meaningful regarding those realities (Mathewes 2008, 34). The entire rationale of confession, for Augustine, is that "the self not only discovers itself but essentially constitutes itself in relation to God" (*conf.* X.32.48). Hence his confession in book X: "To you, then, Lord, I lie exposed, exactly as I am" (*conf.* X.2.2).

God is therefore neither some definitive answer that reveals the unanswerable dimensions of human being nor some projected object of desire through which we can fill in the gaps of our theoretical systems. Rather, for Augustine, God is the ground and excess of our desires—that which is beyond our own descriptive capacities. And to speak of that God both prior to and independent of us therefore requires making use of borrowed language of desire and sensuality (Williams 2016a, 9). As Rowan Williams has insightfully deciphered, the very attempt to speak of God in *The Confessions* is aimed at shining a light on our own incompleteness. I am, simply put, inevitably incomplete and therefore incapable of remembering or speaking God properly or completely. Whatever unity Augustine finds in himself in this act of confession, then, is distinctively not based in himself. He confesses, Williams explains, "in the hope of receiving a unity constructed not by human words and human power (a unity which doesn't therefore need to be *defended* by the anxious and violent deployment of words and power) but by the divine act of seeing and hearing (or reading)" (Williams 2016a, 9).

The issue, for Augustine, is not that a finite, time-bound individual is altogether incapable of moving from ignorance to knowledge or addressing the infinite God; quite the opposite, in fact. Augustine insists that given how obscure we are to ourselves, we can only come to understand something of the sorts of beings we are by passing through the infinity of God (Williams 2016a, 4). That is, coming to know myself requires coming to know God from within the boundaries of an existence marked by time, space, and finitude—hence Augustine's theoretical investigation of the confusions of time in *The Confessions* (Williams 2016a, 4). Being in time is a rather perplexing phenomenon, after all. To be in time is to be a creature tending toward nonbeing (*conf.* XI.14.17). Or, in a proto-Heideggerian sense, to be is to be on a timeline toward death. For Augustine, the elusive passage of time (from anticipation of the future to present experience and into a past accessible only by way of my unreliable memory) perfectly signifies the fragility of time-conditioned creatures (*conf.* XI.14.17). As Augustine notes, "I have come to the conclusion that time is nothing other than tension: but tension of what, I do not know, and I would be very surprised if it is not tension of consciousness itself" (*conf.* XI.26.33). It makes some sense, then, that he goes on to speak of the whole of one's life and actions in terms of the reading of a poem, as we shift from expectation to memory by way of a rapidly successive series of present moments, gone just as quick as they come (*conf.* XI.28.38). The self, in time, is an altogether unstable entity.

There is no selfhood, then, that is entirely under the control of that self. Whatever coherence is to be arrived at in regards to my status or meaning as a creature before God is necessarily given by

God as a listener and observer who is carefully, patiently "reading" the text that is my life.[1] And as Williams points out, this means that the meaning of whatever is written—whatever becomes of my life—is, in the end, not finally determined by me. The ultimate meaning and horizon of creaturely life is not "available for human inspection." I simply cannot reach the perspective from which it all makes sense or adds up. Hence the ways my own narration of my past experiences change so frequently. Coming to know myself truthfully entails coming to terms with absence—of God as an object of knowledge, with the final horizon from which I can make sense of my self, and with the possibility of any complete, finished sense of selfhood (Williams 2016a, 5). In this sense, Augustine's anthropology can be most coherently understood in terms of narrative and textuality. And God, within such a framework, is the divine source of my text who is simultaneously reading and coherently interpreting the various pieces of my life that remain so elusive to me. God is the "infinite attention" to me that remains beyond my own control and limit (Williams 2016a, 10).

This is, importantly, for Augustine, not an alienating reality. Such an approach stems from one's need and desire to come to terms with their finitude and materiality. There is no stepping outside of or above language and time. Suffering absence, in this sense, is coming to terms with the nature of our own being. Augustine is painting a picture of a self "more passive than active," whose most constitutive experience is being given its life rather than creating it for itself. But that being also actively participates in the construction of that life, and they do so most humanely in the act of confession—in response to the confounding mystery that is the gift of being and grace given by the God governing that life and patiently reading that narrative (Mathewes 2008, 65).

A coherent picture of the self and realistic interpretation of God's presence and absence is only possible, then, in the wake of coming to terms with otherness lying at the very heart and core of the self (Mathewes 2008, 71). The best place to make sense of both the wide range of activities that make up a human life and the otherness lying

---

[1]This metaphor is widely acknowledged in Augustinian Studies, and particular attention is given to Augustine's use of the metaphor in the first book of *Confessions*. See Mathewes 2003; Williams 2016a; Stock 1996.

at the core of that human is the soul. And in unifying these themes, the capacities of the soul are key for uncovering an Augustinian understanding of work.

On the Soul of the Animal Who Works

The Capacities of the Soul

In shifting to a discussion of some (seemingly obtuse) technical details of the soul, though, we must remember two important points. The first is the broader context of Augustine's anthropology. This technical investigation of the soul is rooted within Augustine's larger anthropological vision. That is, he is not interested in detailing the soul for the sake of the soul as much as in investigating the nature of the soul given the crucial role it plays in animating the life of the human and enabling our knowing and loving God. The second point to remember is the primary aim of this chapter—I am working to articulate the nature and function of work within Augustine's theological anthropology. In order to locate the role of work in that theological system, we must now turn to a technical analysis of the human soul in order to (1) explicate the nature of the activity that is work, (2) understand why it is a uniquely human phenomenon within Augustine's system, and (3) place the activity in relation to the other, more pressing activities of the soul (i.e., knowing and loving God).

According to Augustine, the soul is crucially bound up in the self's pursuit of God precisely because the mind is said to be the rational capacity of the soul (Bruno Niederbacher 2014, 125–6). The soul is, immaterial, while the corruptible body perishes (*Trin.* X.7.9). Most simply, the soul is what animates the body. The human being is constituted as a soul and body composite, and the human soul is rational in nature (Bruno Niederbacher 2014, 125). The Trinitarian structure of the mind—memory, understanding, and will/love—is itself rooted in the broader entity Augustine refers to as "the soul." As such, the soul is made in the image of God because the soul makes possible the human's proximity to and search for God (*quant.* 33.70; Bruno Niederbacher 2014, 125).

Given that the soul is what animates the body, Augustine thinks that animals have souls much like humans do. In fact, he thinks that all living things (plant life included) contain a soul, though he also insisted those souls differ in important ways (Bruno Niederbacher 2014, 125). Augustine develops a hierarchy of sorts in order to highlight the extent to which the human soul resembles and diverges from other souls. Rather than thinking of these as discrete levels or areas of the soul, though, we must recognize Augustine's treatment revolving around various powers or functions that different souls may or may not be capable of carrying out.

The most basic function—shared by plants, animals, and humans alike—is animation. In this state, the soul gives life to the body and animates its physiological survival according to the nature of its body. He notes, "these [powers] can be seen to be common to man with plants; for we say of them too that they love; we see and we acknowledge that everyone of them is kept and is nourished and grows and germinates each in its own kind" (*quant.* 189–91). Whether in plants, dogs, or humans, the soul here is said to perform functions like distribute nourishment, enable regeneration, and keep the material form of the body intact. The second, more complex function is sensation. He is imagining the ability to feel and distinguish texture, temperature, and weight as well as hearing, smelling, and seeing. Additionally, this second level of sensation refers to appetition and movement, which function in tandem. Sexuality and the ability to care for offspring also emerge here, along with memory and habit (*quant.* 191–3). Even still, all such forms of agency fall within the broader animal category (*quant.* 193).

It is only after reaching the third level of the soul's capacities that Augustine speaks of something uniquely human. Whereas the souls of plants, animals, and humans are capable of animation, only the human soul, Augustine argues, is capable of the following higher functions. Discursive reasoning refers to the soul's capacity for cultural invention in art, language, counting, writing, organization, law, and so on (*quant.* 193–5; Bruno Niederbacher 2014, 126). He speaks of craftsmanship and the preservation of memory in writing, play, music, conjecture, and argumentation. And "this abounding property common to [rational] souls is shared in degrees by the learned and the unlearned, by the good and the bad" (*quant.* 195).

The fourth level, *virtus*, is evaluative and ethical (Bruno Niederbacher 2014, 126). Morality becomes a determining factor here, and *virtus* enables metaphysical reflection (*quant.* 197). This matters because *virtus* allows one to see the differences between oneself purified and oneself defiled. We are capable of comparing goods, following moral statutes, and undergoing moral transformation due to this particular function of the soul. The fifth capacity of the soul is *tranquillitas* (rest). This is the level at which one's fears and anxieties (typically regarding death) are overcome. Once freed from sins and living a holy life, *tranquillitas* enables the contemplation of and advancement toward God, which Augustine treats as its own kind of work (*quant.* 199). The sixth level—*ingressio* (entering)—drives one to (and enables) an understanding of the deepest level of things. And the final, seventh level of *contemplatio* represents the culmination of that desire. This refers to the soul's contemplation and engagement with truth and goodness itself—God as the cause of all things. It is in that encounter that one's experience with truth culminates (*quant.* 203–5).

It is important to note here that Augustine's treatment revolves around various powers or functions that different souls may or may not be capable of carrying out; the issue is not whether the capacities are always or even regularly directed toward God in the way Augustine thinks most fitting. Just consider the frequency by which he takes himself to be improperly loving God (and therefore himself and the world) in *The Confessions*. That is, while it is fitting for the soul to be directed toward God, it regularly is not. This, however, does not shift Augustine's conception of himself as a person. That is, even when one's soul is not properly directed toward God, one continues having the same agential capacities (stemming from their soul) that make them a person. Proper love and worship of God is made possible through the human soul's capacities, and the capacities do not disappear when they are not directed toward God. In a technical and important sense, each person has the capacity for discursive reasoning (the soul's capacity for cultural invention in art, language, counting, writing, organization, law, craftsmanship, the preservation of memory in writing, play, music, conjecture, and argumentation.), *virtus* (evaluative and ethical), *transquillitas* (rest, overcoming fears and anxieties), *ingressio* (entering, driving one to an understanding of the deepest level of understanding of things), and *contemplatio* (contemplation of and engagement with truth and goodness itself) even when they are not contemplating the triune God.[2]

Augustine scholar Edmund Hill has argued that none of this qualifies as any sort of new, innovative claim about the nature of the soul. Augustine is much more interested in noting its function than he is in defining its nature (Hill 2012, 324). He starts with the insight that the soul—or the mind, as he sometimes calls the particular function of the soul he finds most interesting and important—is the source of self-awareness. The soul enables reflexivity. The soul knows itself—it loves itself, as he goes to great lengths to demonstrate in the latter half of *The Trinity*—"simply by being itself," as Hill explains (Hill 2012, 324). Working outward from that center, Augustine builds up the *psyche* as a collection of interrelated functions (see more on this further). It is open to God above and within itself, and it receives the bodily senses from below and outside itself.

The Animal that Works

Within that schema, the human's being, structure, and bodily nature cannot be understood apart from its most basic animal functions. Indeed, many of the defining characteristics of our humanity are, in fact, functions of the soul that we share with other animals. For example, all animals have five senses, and this enables something quite like sense knowledge (*quant.* 137–9; *Trin.* XI.27). All animals, he explains, have some form of memory, sensation, and will—how else would a bird be able to trace its way back to its nest after each outing? (*conf.* X.17.26). Animals are driven by an instinct for survival, and they actively work to avoid death (*civ. Dei.* XI.27). He even thinks that humanity's linguistic capacities fall, to some extent,

---

[2]This matters given the way in which the category of "worship" was used as a legitimating litmus test in colonial and genocidal practices of Native American populations, for instance. It flies in the face of Augustine's theological anthropology to suggest that a person stops being a person if and when they do not worship God. And, if one is to actually follow Augustine in his theological ethics, the proper contemplation and enjoyment of God dictates a particular love of other humans (and animals) that stands to confront that history of classification, genocide, and extinction.

within the broader animal category (*doc. Chr.* II.2.3). Augustine develops a theological anthropology wherein the human is classified as a particular sort of "animal" (fraught as contemporary theorists have shown this sweeping category to be).

It is quite clear for Augustine, though, that none of this qualifies animals as rational creatures (*civ. Dei.* I.20; *quant.* 139). Animals can sense, remember, and seek what is pleasurable to them, but Augustine thinks they are incapable of "taking note of such things" due to their lack of reason. "Taking note" refers to a mode of complex analysis made possible by higher form of reasons such as judgment and evaluation (*Trin.* XII.2,2). And so, as was typical for his time and context, Augustine argued that animals do not have rational knowledge; they act according to sense perception, which he took to be something quite different than rational knowledge (*quant.* 155–7). He even goes so far as to wonder in *The City of God* (though he never definitively answers the question) if an animal's action "by which they act according to their nature in seeking or shunning something" can actually be said to stem from a will at all (*civ. Dei.* V.9).

Human beings, on the other hand, are said to be distinct from their animal others in their intellect.[3] Augustine rendered the human as a rational, mortal, and grammarian animal (*quant.* 137). We are reasoning, thinking, choosing, comprehending, loving animals, and no other animal, Augustine argues, is capable of such intellectual

---

[3] It should be noted here that Augustine's treatment of "animal arationality" is but an assumption, and it is arguably a faulty one. There is a growing body of evidence suggesting the possibility of animal language and varied modes of understanding in animal cognition. The point here is that the question remains emphatically undecided in contemporary scientific research, though Augustine (quite characteristically for his time, we must remember) treats the issue as a certain fact. That said, I do not perceive my proposals to hinge on any particular answers to those research questions. Should Augustine's assumptions about the unique capacities of human beings be proven correct, for example, my argument regarding the nature of work as a uniquely human phenomenon would stand unchallenged. And if Augustine's presumptions are ever proven false, the category I am investigating (i.e. animals that work) would merely be expanded. And the human animal would still face the same challenges and questions regarding the nature, meaning, limits, and end of their work. As such, as interested as I am in the question(s) regarding animal language and cognition, the status of their answers would have little impact on the proposals articulated in this book.

agency. Humanity's unique intellectual capacities have powerful implications too—they make possible our knowing God and ourselves. In this act of rational self-reflection, Augustine explains that we have entered into uniquely human territory (*conf.* X.25.36). The ability to question—even to question myself—leads to a unique capacity for understanding, which, for Augustine, correlates to our ability to "glimpse the unseen things of God" (*conf.* X.6.10).

While the capacity for reason and understanding is what separates us from the other animals with which we roam the world, Augustine thinks there is a real necessity to and goodness in these more basic animal functions. It is not as though an animal's inability to think rationally—their incapacity for really understanding something like Euclidean geometry, for example—establishes any moral lack. Augustine's model simply takes these animals to be arational rather than irrational. Animals act according to their created nature, and they were not created as rational creatures. Nonetheless, they are definitively good within that order of creation. Each creature is seen to contribute to the larger order "in proportion to the just beauty and the arrangement of all things" (*quant.* 215). So too with humans—the functions and agential capacities we share with these other animals are neither debased nor accidental. Rather, these capacities actually play a crucial role in our being human. And Augustine thinks they play a crucial role in moving us toward our ultimate calling of knowing and loving God. Our progressive formation into the eternity, truth, and charity of God cannot be carried out apart from our animalistic urges, our sense-perceptions, and our being embodied in time. Hence the import of our animal natures—much of our agency is crucially directed to our survival, "to the utilizations of changeable and bodily things without which this life cannot be lived" (*Trin.* XII.13.21).

The catch, for Augustine, is that we are not the sort of animals whose final calling or ultimate destiny is contained within the plane of bodily survival. These animal phenomena and functions simply cannot deliver our happiness. And so the task becomes discerning how we are to make use of those drives unto our pursuit of truth, beauty, and the love of God, which cannot occur apart from our being in the world. We do this "in order to do whatever we do in the reasonable use of temporal things with an eye to the acquisition of eternal things, passing by the former on the way, setting our hearts on the latter to the end" (*Trin.* XII.13.21).

Augustine's *psyche* is divided into two parts, and each part contains its own subdivision. The inner part consists of *sapientia* (the contemplation of the eternal) and *scientia* (rational judgment and decisions regarding temporal realities), and the outer part consists of higher (memory/imagination) and lower (sensation) functions. Throughout *De Trinitate*, Augustine uses three different words to name these various psychic functions. *Mens* refers to the 'mind,' though with it he refers to the higher psychic functions (volitional, affective, cognitive) that ultimately make possible *scientia* and *sapientia*. *Mens* is, practically speaking, synonymous with the inner person. He uses *mens humana* to refer to the whole psychic structure (inner and outer). *Animus* is the second word he uses quite frequently. It is a broader term that, Hall explains, "stands for the human soul precisely as rational, and could never be used for the souls or life principles of animals," Hall translates *animus* as "consciousness." *Anima* is translated as "soul," but Augustine regularly urges us to remember that he is not uniquely referring to the human soul with the term. But, once again, Augustine's not very precise and regular in his use of this term either. It is not as though he uses it to refer to the outer functions alone. This is why, *mens* can be said to refer to the inner functions, *animus* to the lower functions, and *anima* to the whole system (Hill 2012).

Within this framework, the inner pursuits (love of God's beauty and truth as made possible by rational capacities) depend on an effective functioning of the outer pursuits (all other animal functions):

> We are dealing with the inner man and that knowledge of his which is about temporal and changeable things. When anything is taken up in pursuit of this knowledge from things that belong to the outer man, it is taken up for the lesson it can provide to foster rational knowledge; and thus the rational use of things we have in common with non-rational animals belongs to the inner man, and cannot properly be said to be common to us and non-rational animals. (*Trin.* XIII.1.4)

Augustine is therefore much more concerned with rational capacities directing us toward God than rational capacity itself. The image of God can therefore be understood, most simply, as the human in search of God (*Trin*). And, for Augustine, that search is largely wrapped up with and animated by the soul's capacities.

With that context in mind, we must now turn to the issue of work as it relates to the function and capacities of the soul.

The Work of the Soul

There have been many efforts to distinguish work from labor, but I will attempt no such undertaking. I am therefore treating "work" as a rationally understood productive activity. To be clear, this is my own definition; Augustine never actually defines the activity as such. And yet, I believe my definition fits his broad use of the term. He speaks of uncompensated activities in the monastic context, professional endeavors, necessary tasks, and work in Eden in similar terms. The slippage between compensated and commodified work helpfully translates to Augustine's treatment of the concept too, as he maintains no strict boundaries between productive activity done in a professional context (commodified and compensated) and work in a communal setting for the sake of perpetuating one's livelihood.

Some might worry that such a definition is problematically broad, but I believe the breadth is precisely what makes this definition tenable. The long history of reproductive labor demonstrates the illegitimacy of coherent distinctions between "work" and "labor." Consider the acts of cooking or caring for children. A chef at a busy restaurant is compensated for the same basic activities that a stay-at-home mother does for free. But this does not categorize the mother's work as something altogether different from the chef's; his is commodified (and therefore compensated work), and hers is not. And, at the same time, both cooks can experience profound moments of joy, pain, service, gratitude, disappointment, and fulfillment in their productive activities. And the economy can depend on, exploit, and celebrate both agents and their productive activity simultaneously.

If work is a catchall term for productive activity, then it clearly depends on a range of functions of the soul. More specifically, this kind of work depends on the first four levels/capacities of Augustine's model of the soul: animation, sensation, discursive reasoning, and evaluative logic (*virtus*). Given that the latter two are uniquely human, it makes sense to claim that the rationally understood component of the definition of work I am positing here positions work as a uniquely human phenomenon.

All of this matters in that this positions work as a function of the human soul. And yet, it demonstrates that work depends on the lowest functions of the soul. It must therefore be undertaken in relation to the higher capacities with which it has little to do: *tranquilitas*, *engressio*, *contemplation*. More specifically, work is made possible by the lower levels of the soul (i.e., animation and sensation), but the meaning and understanding of that work, which makes possible a proper relation to it, depends on the higher functions of the soul. Given that the inner pursuits (love of God's beauty and truth as made possible by rational capacities) depend on an effective functioning of the outer pursuits (work, in this case), the ethical task for the believer hoping to work faithfully is to orient and undertake their work in service of the flourishing of their inner needs.

Conclusion: Defining Work and Its End

The task of this first chapter was to situate work in relation to the final end of the human—knowing and loving God—in and through an exploration of the capacities of the soul. Work's nature and meaning are only legible in relation to the human being's purpose, nature, and place within the order of creation. I have attempted to demonstrate this by analyzing the metaphor of work and through an investigation of work as a function of the soul, which is always already aimed at higher ends.

In order to connect work with that final end, I began with an extended analysis of one of Augustine's most frequent metaphors for the life of the Christian: work. He regularly phrases our eschatological encounter with God in terms of rest and our struggle to conform ourselves to Christ during our lives in the world in terms of toilsome labor. The final end for which the human is aiming—final union God in the end—is characterized as a form of rest. That rest, Augustine believes, stems from our proximity to God, who is the abundant, loving source of all goodness and existing things. Hoping in that restful end, Augustine believes, should transform the way we experience toil while we are in the world. We are to toil faithfully, patiently now in hope of the coming rest. This metaphor (i.e., the growth of the life of the Christian as a kind of work), highlighting toil and struggle as it does, tells us a few key things about Augustine's understanding of our time during the world: the way we currently experience work is the result of sin (and therefore quite different than whatever counted as work in Eden); we have been given the grace to choose better ends and faithfully navigate a fallen world, even now; work will be eschatologically abolished; and hoping in that end should transform the way in which we undertake that toilsome activity during our lives in the world. Put simply, we are to work now in light of the end toward which we are headed: being in God.

I defined work in terms of rationally understood productive activity. As such, work depends on a wide range of the soul's functions: work is made possible by the lower levels of the soul (i.e., animation and sensation), but the meaning and understanding of that work, which makes possible a proper relation to it, depends on the higher functions of the soul. The ethical task for the believer hoping to work faithfully is to orient and undertake their work in service of the flourishing of their inner needs.

Impossible as it might seem, the task of this book is to deploy the latent resources of Augustine for the sake of navigating those demands as faithfully as possible. In order to do so, we must now turn toward a fuller treatment of the nature of work in the garden before examining the effects of sin on work. Only then might we come to understand the full scope of challenges before us. Thankfully Augustine has much to offer on both counts.

2

Working the Garden

Introduction

For Augustine, work's value and dignity stem from creation. In the creation narratives, humans find a certain obligation to work. That is, the injunction to work—to care for and perpetuate themselves—did not stem from the fall. Rather, Augustine reminds his readers that humanity labored in the garden prior to the fall, even if that work was qualitatively different than what workers experience today. Work was no hardship in the garden; it was more akin to a spontaneous experience of joy grounded in creaturely agency. On this point Augustine writes,

> The things created by God grew more exuberantly and fruitfully through the concurrent labor of man, resulting in more copious praise of the Creator himself who had given to a soul consigned to an animal body the intellect and faculty of rational activity in proportion to the willingness of the spirit, and not in proportion to the necessity of satisfying the needs of the body. (*Gn. litt.* XVIII.8)

And examining the nature of that work in the garden tells us something important about both the confluence of agencies that make humans' work possible and the role that work is to play in the life of the person before God.

In light of that, the basic task of this chapter is to assemble and analyze Augustine's understanding of prelapsarian work so as to (1) articulate the confluence of creaturely and divine agency in all human work (i.e., pre- and postlapsarian) and (2) to use those insights to speak to the role that work should play in the lives of Christians today.

In order to accomplish those goals, I will draw heavily on Augustine's various commentaries on Genesis, as these are the texts in which Augustine gives his most detailed, sustained treatments of work in Eden. Because Augustine's approach to biblical texts is largely either unknown or foreign to contemporary readers, I begin this chapter with a brief orientation to Augustine's hermeneutical strategy and reading of Genesis, which frames the three commentaries I will draw on in this chapter: *De Genesi as Litteram* (*The Literal Meaning of Genesis*), *De Genesi as Litteram Liber Imperfectus* (*Unfinished Literal Commentary on Genesis*), and *De Genesi adversus Manichaeos* (*On Genesis: A Refutation of the Manichees*). In beginning with Augustine's approach to the text, I hope to clarify to readers the means by which we might read and think about the contemporary implications of this ancient Scriptural text. Doing so, I believe, should clarify (1) why I believe (along with Augustine) that drawing contemporary implications from this highly contested, ancient text is a worthwhile endeavor; (2) how we ought to understand our own limited interpretations in the process; (3) how my own understanding of the historicity of Adam (or lack thereof) diverges from Augustine's; and (4) what the implications of those divergences mean for thinking about work in the garden.

After addressing the hermenutical issues, I then turn to Augustine's analysis of work in the garden. I organize and synthesize the scattered passages wherein Augustine treats the question of prelapsarian work so as to articulate his understanding of the nature, meaning, and experience of that work. Given Adam and Eve's lack of perishability, their work was not intended to cultivate food required for their survival. It was, rather, an integrated mode of creaturely engagement within a complex, ordered ecosystem that simply was creation. Undertaken in this manner, Adam and Eve's work was aimed at (1) the discovery of their immediate relation to God as the source of all being, (2) the discovery of the types of creatures they were in relation to the larger order in which they found themselves, and (3) a contributive, participatory mode of engagement wherein they investigated, engaged with, and built on God's good, multilayered creation, all of which Augustine believes was particularly honoring to the creator God. Put differently, this work was an active, embodied mode of knowledge.

In his treatment of work in Eden, Augustine articulates a few key mechanics about the God–world relation and the nature of human agency in relation to the divine. These insights about the interrelation of human and divine agencies were true of Adam and Eve prior to the fall, and they true are for you and me now. As such, they tell us something important about how our work is always already related to God's own agency, even today. In the third section of this chapter, I will bring this Augustinian vision of agency into conversation with Kathryn Tanner's constructive theology, so as to elucidate what is implied in Augustine's treatment of work in Eden and to clarify the ways in which our work is—even today— always already part and parcel of God's agency. God, being more present to us than we are ourselves, is simultaneously the source of all existence and the immanent presence of that existence. When articulated in this manner, human and divine agencies are seen as compatible when we consider God's agency as the foundation and ground of human being rather than some sort of suppression of that active potential (Tanner 2004, 82–90). The collaborative work of Adam and Eve finding their place in creation and tending to the garden—through the intellectual powers and active agencies—was thus a unique, honoring mode of encountering God in and through their own creative agencies.

After exploring the relation between these two modes of agency, I then conclude the chapter with a brief reflection on how and why these insights should matter for the ways we work today.

Reading Augustine Reading Genesis

Reading Genesis

Given my goal of analyzing work in Eden, we will be spending some time in Augustine's commentaries on Genesis. Before diving into the work-specific details, it is worth noting some of how Augustine reads Genesis. That is, in order to get as much out of his treatment of work in Eden, we first need to attune ourselves to the ways he reads Genesis as a complex, dynamic text.

Augustine was consistently drawn to the question of creation for a number of telling reasons. To begin with, he felt that properly treating Genesis—that is, doing the text's nuances and myriad literal/figurative meanings justice—was an exegetical challenge *par excellence*. Developing such a commentary would put his highest intellectual capacities to the test (Hill 2004, 13).

But he was drawn to Genesis for more existential reasons as well. His prioritization of the relationship between God and himself (as a creature) inevitably led him back to the mystery of creation. But this was not merely the final stopping point in tracing the details of a reversed timeline; rather, Augustine also understood that the nature of God's relation to creation underlies every religious act and expression. For Augustine, as we previously established, one only ever thinks, does, moves, or has their being in relation to the creator. The human's freedom and ability to choose is totally, absolutely dependent on the God that is Being itself, who freely gives life to creatures in an ongoing way. Creation thus refers to the originary act whereby God gives existence to things outside of God, but it also refers to the continued ways that God preserves created reality at all. Hence the fertile ground Augustine perceived the doctrine to be (Hill 2004, 14–15).

This is also why the exploration of creation begins with Genesis but must go beyond that text. Augustine himself frequently departs from that which is directly raised by the text to speculatively explore the swath of truths raised by the text. To think with Genesis about the act of creation and the God–world relation requires we think with Genesis beyond Genesis (Hill 2004, 16).

This is no simple task, particularly when one (as Augustine did) tries to balance the layered meanings of any given passage: literal, figurative, spiritual, and so on. Given the challenge, fragility, and speculative nature of such interpretive gestures, Augustine frames his interpretations and conclusions to us as hypotheses— incomplete and partially conjectural. That is, the text raises more questions than it gives definitive answers to, and so we must remember the speculative, conjecture-based nature of our own interpretations.

More specifically, Augustine believed that good Scriptural interpretation should be undertaken with humility and in conjunction with the norm of faith. Reason and faith were thus both required. The interpreter must ensure she is not overconfidently proposing meanings and ideas that betray the coherency of the faith and text(s), and she must avoid positioning her own interpretative conjectures (carefully arrived at as they might be) as definitively true, as though the meaning of the text could be so easily consumed, packaged, and redeployed (Augustine 2004b, 106).

Even still, those hypotheses can and should drive us toward the divine mystery. In reading Genesis, Augustine was most concerned to highlight the existential issues raised by the mystery of creation and the relations implied in such a phenomenon (Hill 2004, 21). As Edmund Hill writes in the introduction to the Genesis commentaries, "The questions which the sacred scriptures raised to the inquiring mind converged ultimately in the unfathomable mystery of God" (Hill 2004, 17). And so we see in his reading of Genesis that a human being becomes more itself—more humane, as it were—in the process of deepening our understanding of the mysteries of creation. This is because investigating creation entails moving into the mystery of the creator itself and situating ourselves within the fabric of the created order, as beloved creatures more fully aware of ourselves and the creator God that continues giving us the gift of life itself. The Genesis commentaries are thus resources for us as readers to live existentially into the mystery of creation (Hill 2004, 21–2). And this is precisely why those commentaries (and Genesis, for that matter) can still speak so fruitfully toward our questions regarding contemporary life.

On the Question of Adam's Historicity

Before I can draw conclusions regarding work in Eden, I need to explain what I mean when I say "Eden." Doing so requires we take up the question of history and the historicity of the Genesis text, most specifically.

Augustine favored a dynamic reading of Genesis. In his typical clarity, he notes his familiarity with a range of interpretations: some readers understand Paradise in a literal sense alone; others take Eden to be a spiritual reality alone; and still some others believe the Genesis texts to speak of both a spiritual and literal Eden. Augustine favors this third option, arguing that while Adam does represent some spiritual phenomena (as Paul speaks of him in terms of an early form of the Christ that would come later), so too does he take the text to speak of a historic person living in a particular time and place. Adam and Eve, he tells us, lived, raised a family, and worked in a real garden in which God placed them (*Gn. litt.* 346).

While Augustine's position on the matter seems coherent enough to me, I do not take it to be either necessary or necessarily authoritative. In fact, Augustine himself has given us the freedom and tools to take a different position on the topic with his idea of interpretations as hypotheses. I certainly cannot give any definitive, objective record of the experience of the first humans, and so my own interpretation follows suit in its hypothetical narrative. And yet, I think careful reading of the meaning of the text requires we make use of the latest information available to us, using that information to aid a rigorous read of this holy writ. Augustine both explicitly urges and models that interpretive strategy.

In what remains of this section, I hope to (very) briefly articulate an alternative read of the Eden narrative, which prioritizes the allegorical meaning of the text so as to rectify the narrative with the insights of evolutionary science and critical historical strategies. Such a reading does not render thinking about work in Eden a meaningless task; quite the opposite, in fact. The text still has much to teach us about the nature of work prior to the fall.

Evolutionary science presents myriad data regarding the progressive emergence of *homo sapiens* from primates, in both archeological and genetic form (Falk 2017). As such, the consensus of our evolutionary history presents something of a challenge for Christian theologies of creation, particualry when one aims to hold onto certain Christian convictions rooted in the biblical narratives and theological tradition: creation out of nothing, the originary goodness of God's creation, and the legitimacy of humanity's sinful state. The biblical narratives present a particular origin narrative, and humanity's scientific engagement with that very created order has presented another. Charles Taylor refers to such tensions as "cross-pressured," meaning that our dual commitment to scripture's authority on our lives and our affirmation of scientific exploration as a legitimate undertaking presents us with two seemingly competing accounts (Cavanaugh and Smith 2017, 11; Taylor 2018).

But as William Cavanaugh and Jamie Smith have demonstrated, these cross-pressured convictions can produce "good problems" that lead to generative developments in Christian theology (Cavanaugh and Smith 2017, 11). Taking the Council of Chalcedon—the fifth-century church council where theologians grappled with the scientific and philosophical challenges of their day within the parameters of Christological development and imaginatively proposed the Chalcedonian definition that insists Christ has two natures in one person—as their model, Smith and Cavanaugh present us with a practical vision of the Christian tradition whose commitments include faithfully extending and interrogating that tradition in light of new philosophical and scientific data (Cavanaugh and Smith 2017, 16; Wells, Lugt, and Wayman 2018). Whatever one takes "the Christian tradition" to be, we must realize that it has taken its present shape in and through these kinds of imaginative, expansive interrogations of developing data. As Smith and Cavanaugh note, "Extension, revision, expansion, and development are intrinsic to the tradition *qua* tradition" (Cavanaugh and Smith 2017, 17).

Engaging with such new scientific or philosophical developments need not mean any kind of unchecked revision of the theological tradition. One must show the ways in which any generative extension fits with the core narratives and commitments of one's theological tradition (Cavanaugh and Smith 2017, 17–18). As with the practice of submitting to Scripture as authoritative, one must (not so simply) do the work of determining again and again precisely what one takes to be authoritative in such a collection of texts. From an Augustinian perspective, Jamie Smith has articulated an "Augustinian package" that can be used to guide such faithful explorations. In his attempt to prioritize and continue affirming (1) the goodness of creation prior to the emergence of evil (i.e., creation was good when God created it and humanity was indeed righteous before falling into sin) and (2) humanity is incapable of willing the good in itself, which points to the need for redemption through unmerited grace as a divine initiative (Smith 2017, 63). And for Smith, the question becomes whether or not one can merge these basic tenants of the biblical texts with the data presented by evolutionary sciences to develop a coherent narrative of creation (Smith 2017, 63).

I, like Smith, find such a narrative both possible and compelling. In a creative thought experiment that treats one plausible narrative of humanity's collective, progressive emergence from the primate family, Smith speaks of the emergence of a population of hominids in an early, collective population. In the thought experiment, God elects this group once it reaches a point of development wherein those hominids are "exhibiting features of emergent consciousness, relational aptitude, and mechanisms of will—in short, when these hominids have evolved to the point of exhibiting moral capabilities" (Smith 2017, 64). The traditional characteristics of Adam's agency and responsibility can be transferred to this early "original humanity," rather seamlessly: they were not perfect, they were able to carry out the mission received from God, they feature a kind of obvious moral immaturity wherein disobedience can be mistaken as a more desirable good than God itself, and so there was no guarantee of their moral success. The garden of Eden becomes the wild of an expansive creation in which they find themselves, and it serves as the arena in which their probationary period is carried out. And there are discernable effects of their fall, both personally and cosmically: humanity shifts, its moral tendencies are solidified somehow, and they now stand in definitive need of God's initiative and grace to rectify their disordered passions (Smith 2017, 65).

In so doing, Smith is able to affirm both parts of the Augustinian package and the evolutionary picture of a large human population at origin. The fall remains a historical (even if not punctiliar) event, with a certain group receiving a commission from God, being good and able to obey that commission, and falling into a state of sinful rebellion through acts of disobedience over a period of time (Smith 2017, 65).

As tangential as this thought experiment might seem, it is quite crucial to the structure of my treatment of work for a number of reasons. First, it demonstrates the legitimacy and viability of making theological sense of Adam and Eve's work in the garden, even if I do take Genesis 1–3 to be an allegorical telling. Second, it provides a constructive update on Augustine's previously articulated method of reading Genesis. This interpretation-as-hypothesis follows his own urge for a kind of Chalcedonian (even if Augustine was writing prior to the council of Chalcedon itself) read that aims to synthesize scriptural interpretations with the latest scientific and philosophical developments. We simply have new data sets that Augustine was obviously not privy to. And third, it holds onto what I take to be some crucial theological commitments (*creation ex nihilo*, the original goodness of creation, a temporal fall) in a way that legitimates the unknown mechanics by which those realities came to pass. Rather creatively, this thought experiment demonstrates the possibility that the most pressing insights of evolutionary science can be gracefully synthesized with a creative rendering of the creation narrative. That possibility is enough for me to go on.

The Nature of Work in the Garden

Value and Dignity

Augustine insisted throughout his theological oeuvre that labor has both dignity and value. And I believe he manages to affirm the dignity of labor without mandating it or denigrating life outside of labor time (Arbesmann 1973, 248 n. 6). It is important to note, though, that he believes labor's value and dignity stem from creation. In the creation narratives, humans find a certain obligation to labor. The injunction to labor did not stem from the Fall (*Gn. adv. Man.* 81–2; Kidwell 2013, 779 n. 6). Rather, Augustine reminds his readers that humanity labored in the garden prior to the Fall, even if that labor was qualitatively different than what laborers experience today (Arbesmann 1973, 249 n. 6).

Augustine also understood the work of Adam and Eve to be "more laudable" than the work we experience in the wake of the fall, even if he never directly articulates the nature of that work *as such*. He writes, "Work in Paradise, I mean to say, is one thing, and work on the land, to which he was condemned after sinning, quite another. In fact, what sort of work it was, is indicated by the addition of *and to guard it*. In the peaceful tranquility, you see, of the life of bliss, where there is no death, work consists entirely in guarding what you hold" (*Gn. adv. Man.* 81).

My primary task in the following section is to fill in the gaps of Augustine's treatment of work in the garden, using his basic conclusions to sketch a more holistic theory of the nature of that work. That is, I am attempting to extend Augustine's brief treatment beyond itself, so as to draw conclusions about the precise nature of that work and its relevancy for our own working lives. In so doing, I will focus on the work of "tending the garden," which depends on both cognitive and bodily activities. I will be treating that tending to the garden as a kind of thoughtful, responsive engagement to what had already been given. In this sense, the emphasis is not on toil or productivity as much as living into and around the goodness and natural processes of creation as they played out in the garden.

In order to clarify the necessarily abstract notions employed here, I will make extended use of the metaphor of an ecosystem, as I take Adam and Eve's tending to the garden to depend on both (1) a rational, critical engagement with the nature of the ecosystem in which they found themselves and (2) an embodied response to that learned information wherein they learn to foster certain forms of plant and animal flourishing within that ecosystem (as living members of it).

Eden's Work as Active Response to Relational Knowledge

The point of the work can't even have been to produce food, as Augustine argues that there was no need for food prior to sin rendering Adam and Eve mortal. The two could not have died from hunger in that state and so the work must point to some other outcome altogether (Augustine 2004a, 236). It was, rather, an integrated mode of creaturely engagement within a complex, ordered ecosystem that simply was creation. It was a uniquely human mode of engagement with that created order, which was rooted in a particular kind of knowledge and naming. The work entailed finding oneself within the ecosystem(s) that is the created order and facilitating the structured patterns and dynamics of that wonderfully wild garden.

Knowledge, it must be said, was more than a storehouse of facts for Augustine. If *sapientia* (or wisdom) is the highest mode of knowledge and takes God as its object, then knowledge is as much about one's relation to the object in question as it is one's understanding of that object. Further, any information about an object only matters to the extent that it impacts and informs one's relation to that object. My knowledge of God directs my love of God, and vice versa. But the same is true of objects within the created order. As Matthew Knotts has helpfully articulated, for Augustine, "knowledge is not so much about moving to some predetermined goal of imposing order on chaos, but allowing ourselves *to see what is already there*, to adjust ourselves in such a way that the images which appear to us cohere into an intelligible whole" (Knotts 2019, xxi). This is a kind of knowledge as reading, as interpreting the world in which one finds oneself. Knotts continues:

> The presence of God is deep within each of us, in particular in virtue of our creation according to the divine image. The source of all being and truth, the summit of all knowledge, is more intimate to us than we are to ourselves. This observation suggests that knowledge is ultimately not only about the acquisition of facts, of 'scientific' knowledge, but is about a continuous, indefinite deepening, something which cannot be conducted according to the techniques of the scientific method (a point which Gadamer and Buber appreciated). (Knotts 2019, 134)

It makes good sense, then, that Knotts frames this in terms of a dynamic of call and response, or a dialogue:

> We are led to see the world not as a realm evacuated of meaning and inertly awaiting out investigative efforts, but as the repository of truths to be uncovered and understood. It implies an interaction of a hermeneutical or interpretive nature. Augustine challenges us to think of the world as like a text. . . . What does the world say, and how do we respond? . . . Once we begin to read the world, what do we learn? We become aware of our contingency, our dependency, in a contemporary idiom, of finitude. What seems like a trivial observation is replete with epistemic significance for Augustine. Creation implies both a reception of being and a response to its source of our won being or our knowing. (Knotts 2019, 111)

Considering humanity's interaction with the created order of which it is a part thus requires we consider what contemporary poet David Whyte refers to as "the conversational nature of reality." And Augustine actually demonstrates his own conversation with creation in *Confessiones* X, where he speaks of inanimate objects conversing with him, confessing, as it were (*conf.* X; Knotts 2019, 70).

To be clear, I am arguing that within Eden, which is to say prior to the fall, work was a kind of attentive (i.e., cognitive) response (i.e., material and action based) to the calling of the world. And that engaged response was uniquely fitting for the human—the upright, rational animal capable of moving, considering, understanding, hearing, and responding to the demands of that complex created order. Work, I am suggesting, was the attentive, action-based response to this form of relational knowledge. It was, as has been stated, less about sustaining one's existence and more about coming to terms with one's place within the created order and fostering the growth of that ecosystem, all of which must have been uniquely pleasing to God, particularly when such active responses were predicated on one's own understanding of the divine act that made that complex set of relations possible.

Consider how, as Miles Hollingworth has noted, Augustine suspected that part of God's purpose(s) in creating humanity was to give voice to a voiceless creation (Hollingworth 2013, 5–6). He viewed all nonhuman creatures as nonlinguistic; their souls simply do not have the capacity for language. As such, the human is the creature capable of commenting on the raw stuff of material creation (*c. Prisc.* 11). It is because humans have been given a voice and language that they are able to respond to the sheer givenness of creation. Humans are able to both pronounce praise and utter thanksgiving (i.e., worship, as we'll see in Chapter 5), and those twin tasks constituted the work of the human in the pre-fallen Eden.

This kind of work, Rowan Williams explains, must be what it means to realize the image of God (Williams 2016f, 173). We turn to God when we engage with the varied multiplicities of the world, all of which have God as their source (Knotts 2019, 97). How could it be otherwise? This is why it matters to Augustine that humanity has the capacity for self-awareness and interrogation of the created order. The ability to investigate, understand, and care for (as a kind of aware, attentive participation with) creation was all grounded in "a sapiential account of human reason as divine illumination" (Knotts 2019, 76).

Aims of Work in Eden

When undertaken in this context, work was an active, embodied mode of knowledge. Undertaken in this manner, Adam and Eve's work was aimed at (1) the discovery of the types of creatures they were in relation to the larger ecosystem in which they found themselves, (2) the discovery of their immediate relation to God as the source of all being, and (3) a contributive, participatory mode of engagement wherein they investigated, engaged with, and built on God's good, multilayered creation, all of which Augustine believes was particularly honoring to the creator God. Let us examine each of these points in turn.

First, work entailed discovering the type of creatures Adam and Eve were in relation to the larger created order in which they found themselves. In a fascinating, revealing passage, Augustine reflects on the delight and spectacle of this kind of human interaction with the created order. What a gift, that the human, as a part of a complex ecosystem, can reflect on that discovery of the mechanics and interworkings of the ecosystem it finds itself within:

> What greater or more wonderful spectacle can there be, after all, or when is human reasonable after a fashion to converse with "The Nature of Things," than when after seeds have been sown, cuttings potted, shrubs planted out, graftings made, each root and seed is questioned, so to say, on what its inner vital force can or cannot do, what helps and what hinders it, what is the range of the inner, invisible power of its own numerical formula, what that of the care bestowed on it from outside? (*Gn. litt.* 357).

And then to perceive, in and through that mode of engagement and discovery, the very lifeforce that sustains and orders the ecosystem itself. We can even consider this in Pauline terms, as Augustine does when he cites the first letter to the Corinthians: "Neither the one who plants nor the one who waters is anything, but only God who gives the growth" (1 Cor. 3:7). The intellect, agency, and placement that makes the work possible is itself a part and parcel of the larger created entity, sustained, as it were, from the outside by God (*Gn. litt.* 357).

Second, this kind of conversation certainly opens up new modes of exchange with the entities of the created order itself, but because God is the very ground of all created entities and agencies, the conversation always inevitably leads back to the creator. From this perspective, attending to the living things of the created order—by which I mean (1) paying sustained attention and (2) engaging out of that attentive space—inevitably entails consideration of God as the creative source of their existence. This is why Knotts believes that created things serve a kind of referential function, "insofar as when we consider them we are led to a knowledge of their creator, which must then develop into praise" (Knotts 2019, 69). This knowledge is a kind of sustained attention, "an acknowledgment, an appreciation, a recognition, a disposition, i.e. allowing oneself to be open to the truth within." And this kind of attentive engagement with the created order leads one back to the Other that is always closer to me than I am to myself: God, who rests at the very core of my being (Knotts 2019, 90). Reckoning with the transcendent God that is always at the core of my being and the ground of the realities with which I interact thus entails coming to see the world anew. And it clarifies Augustine's goal of perceiving each existent in terms of the overall unity of God's created order. "The act of properly judging material reality in light of its source is itself contemplation. The things of the world, when recognized for what they are, act as so many steps (*gradus*) to eternal and immutable things" (Knotts 2019, 94–5).

Third, this work was uniquely honoring in and through its participatory, humane functioning. That is, the work entailed a kind of symphony of human capacities and activities—bodily movement, sense, rational thought, response—that Augustine believes were uniquely honoring to God precisely because they were uniquely human. The work, in this sense, depends on a combination of properly ordered cognitive and bodily actions. And whatever delights we might now find in agriculture, we must acknowledge that the experiences of the garden were exponentially richer and "more complete" when there were no natural barriers to the intended outcomes of the garden's processes. He writes, "You see, there was no stress of wearisome toil but pure exhilaration of spirit, when things which God had created flourished in more luxuriant abundance with the help of human work" (*Gn. litt.* 356). And this phenomenon must have been a unique pleasure for God, such that the animal that the human is had the physical and rational capacities to work in ways that facilitated the natural processes and was itself an experience of joy—a clear recognition and delight in the pure givenness of creation and its structures. As we see in Jesus' triumphant entry into Jerusalem, the very material of the created order will surely render its praise in and through its being itself, but the praise of the human is a secondary, honoring melody when properly articulated (Luke 19). The work was honoring to God because of the ways Adam and Eve exhibited their creaturely capacities within the heart of a responsive, complex creaturely order, contributing in sync with God as the ground of their agency, all of which was beautiful and fitting. It was all the more honoring to God that it be done this way because God created the creature in such a way that they could contribute in sync with God.

This is precisely why Augustine refers to work in the garden as an experience of "uplift" and "spontaneous joy." As Augustine notes in *De Genesi ad litteram*,

> The things created by God grew more exuberantly and fruitfully through the concurrent work of man, resulting in more copious praise of the Creator himself who had given to a soul consigned to an animal body the intellect and faculty of rational activity in proportion to the willingness of the spirit, and not in proportion to the necessity of satisfying the needs of the body. (*Gn. litt.* VIII.8)

Confluence of Agencies

While we do not experience work in all of those ways today (for reasons we will examine in detail in the next chapter, when we examine the effects of sin on our work), much of what Augustine says about our agency in relation to God's still holds true for us even now. Given that, the nature of work in the garden can tell us something important about both the confluence of agencies that make humans' work possible and the role that work is to play in the life of the person before God.

For Augustine, God is—simultaneously—the source of all existence and the immanent presence of that existence. Augustine's vision of God's transcendence and immanence thus exist in dialectical relation to one another (Mathewes 2008, 83). God, not being affected by the malleable, finite conditions of creaturely change and time, is the life through which we come to know existence at all (Mathewes 2004, 206–7). God, in God's freedom from the imperfect, corrosive forms of mutability that characterize our lives in the world, is the very ground of our being in the world.

Hence, God is more present to us than we are ourselves (*conf.* III.6.11). This is why the continuities and discontinuities between God and creation—that is, God's dialectical transcendence and immanence—are so difficult to separate and articulate in Augustine's theological system. As Rowan Williams has fruitfully summarized, "The continuities, the ways in which creation shares in the sort of life that is God's, steer us inexorably back to the fundamental difference" (Williams 2016b, 67).

Rather than sketching a distant God operating on humans from above, Augustine argues that God is "most high, most deep, and yet nearer than all else, most hidden yet intimately present" (*conf.* VI.4). God is thus "more intimately present to me than my innermost being" (*conf.* 1.1). God's transcendence and immanence operate altogether apart from any distance or measure of space; God is "both interior to every single thing, because *in him are all things* (Rom. 11:36), and exterior to every single thing because he is above all things" (Hill 2004, VIII.26, 48; p. 374). That is, God is the uncaused cause all existing things (*civ. Dei.* V.9). This is why Augustine asks, "And whence would it have any kind of being, if not from you, from whom derive all things which to any degree have being?" (*conf.* XI.7.7). God is the very ground and cause of creaturely agency rather than some extra agent in the same causal plane.[1]

It is for this reason that Charles Mathews has identified resonances between this Augustinian framework and Kathryn Tanner's vision of classical transcendence: "God's creative action upon the world, and the action of created agents within it, thus operate on two different logical levels; they are, in Kathryn Tanner's formulation, 'noncontrastive'" (Mathewes 2004, 206, footnote 26). This dialectical sketch of transcendence/immanence thus serves as a helpful, critical tool through which we can guard against theological treatments that "implant God too immanently within the world and those that remove God too transcendently from it"

---

[1]It should be clear that I do not intend to frame this vision of transcendence and divine agency as a uniquely Augustinian phenomenon. Rather, Augustine articulates a classical vision of transcendence that is arguably shared by a host of other theologians scattered throughout the Christian intellectual tradition. I merely mean to use Augustine as a way into that vision and to draw on his understanding of the implications of that vision for theological anthropology.

(Mathewes 2004, 207). For Augustine and Tanner alike, traditional claims about God and creation are rectified and made coherent by avoiding either of those outcomes.

Tanner points to a consistency of talk about the Christian creator God's transcendence and subsequently demonstrates the consistency of that speech with the notion of creaturely agency (Tanner 2004, 36). She turns to Hellenistic and Greek philosophies in order to highlight the tensions operative in claims regarding a transcendent God who is also involved in the world. Such claims do not tend to hang together well. The root of the problem, though, lies in the way contrastive theories of transcendence posit God in terms of opposition to the created world, as one being among others of a singular order (Tanner 2004, 45). This approach limits God by opposing it to that which God is said to create. Within such a structure, God's influence and agency are necessarily limited like the other finite agents God is said to stand in relation to.

While Tanner much prefers the non-contrastive vision she identifies in Plotinus, from whom she begins to develop her theory of noncompetition, a similar approach is identifiable with Augustine's treatment of the same cluster of concepts. If God is the source of all, then God cannot be compared to or characterized in terms of the beings which depend on God for existence (Tanner 2004, 43). Non-contrastive transcendence posits a God radically involved in the world, whose agency extends over every form of action as its source of being. This extreme form of divine involvement depends on a radical form of transcendence (Tanner 2004, 46). The one mandates and depends upon the other. Tanner thus, first, articulates particular rules by which coherent theological speech should operate: "avoid both a simple univocal attribution of predicates to God and world and a simple contrast of divine and non-divine predicates" (Tanner 2004, 47). Second: "Avoid in talk about God's creative agency all suggestions of limitation in scope or manner. The second rule prescribes talk of God's creative agency as immediate and universally extensive" (Tanner 2004, 47). Such rules help to make Christian theological speech both coherent and consistent.

Whereas contrastive forms of transcendence posit God in terms of opposition to the created world, as one being among others of a singular order, non-contrastive transcendence posits a God radically involved in the world. Within this framework,

God's agency extends over every form of action as its source of being. God's difference from creatures depends on God's direct involvement with every aspect of their being (Tanner 2004, 39–57). God is thus the transcendental ground of human consciousness and subjectivity, and creaturely being becomes what it is by depending on God. As Tanner notes, "There need be no contradiction in saying relations that are free or contingent along the horizontal axis of created order are determined to be so in a vertical relation of absolute dependence upon divine agency" (Tanner 2004, 90). When articulated in this manner, human and divine agencies are seen as compatible when we consider God's agency as the foundation and ground of human being rather than some sort of suppression of that active potential (Tanner 2004, 82–90).

This is precisely why Augustine does not see any sort of tension between divine and human agencies, distinct as they might be. In fact, he even recognizes a certain form of correlation between the two agencies since they do not operate competitively within a singular causal plane. Given the nature of God's creation and preservation—God's continual, generous giving of being to all existing things—Augustine insists that it is God that grows agricultural goods, even if through the phenomenon of human work (Hill 2004, 5.6.18; 285). It is for good reason that we do not treat farmers as the sole creators of their crops; farmers actualize a creative process—potentiality—that exists outside of their own capacities and within the created order itself. God, Augustine reminds his readers, is the ground of that creative potential and process—not the farmer. He notes, "It is through the external action [of those farmers] that the power of God operates inwardly to create these things" (*Trin.* III.8.13). That is, God's will is accomplished in material creation by producing effects in and through free creaturely agents (*Trin.* III.1.6). All created bodies are subject to the will of God precisely in that they have no power, being, or agency apart from what God continually grants them. No act of human agency can therefore occur independently of God's will (*Trin.* III.1.7). Thus "God's will is the first and highest cause of all physical species and motions" (*Trin.* III.1.4, 9). God's creative form of action can thus be said to be the sourcing and empowerment of creaturely agency in the fullness of its creative potential (*civ. Dei.* V.9).

Conclusion: Eden's Implications

A careful reading of Augustine's commentaries on Genesis provided us with a complex, compelling vision of the nature of work in Eden. This toil-free work was experienced as all joy, and it served drastically different purpose than our work today. Rather than working to sustain themselves and perpetuate their existence, Adam and Eve's work served to (1) clarify to them the nature of God as the source of their being, (2) discover their place within a larger, complex ecosystem, and (3) honor God by exhibiting their human capacities within that ordered ecosystem. When undertaken in this capacity, Adam and Eve's work was a kind of embodied knowledge, fully activated within the order of creation and thereby very pleasing to God, the creator and sustainer of all.

For Augustine, Genesis was not merely an abstract puzzle or intellectual problem to be worked out. The text certainly presented intellectual problems and conceptual challenges, but the challenges were navigated because of the text's potential relevancy. He was driven to the text by existential concerns, and a careful engagement with the text led him to a deeper understanding of himself, his place in God's created order, and further into the mysteries of God. I have lingered on the nature of work in Eden for similar reasons, with similar hopes of clarifying something about our work, our place within God's created order, and the mysteries of God.

And so the question remains: What should this vision of work in the garden of Eden mean for working people today? This vision of work in Eden helps clarify the final end of work (i.e., its *telos*), our immediate relation to God in work, and the effects of sin on our work today.

Our experience of work (as we will explore in the next chapter) today is drastically different than work in Eden due to the effects of sin. And yet even the damaging effects of sin have not undone or reoriented the final ends of work that we see in Eden. Human work was (and remains) honoring to God precisely because of the conglomeration of agencies exhibited in the activity.

Examining the nature of work in Eden has also clarified something of the nature of our agency *as such*. God, being more present to us than we are ourselves, is simultaneously the source of all existence and the immanent presence of that existence. When articulated in this manner, human and divine agencies are seen as compatible when we consider God's agency as the foundation and ground of human being rather than some sort of suppression of that active potential (Tanner 2004, 82–90). And as we saw in Augustine's treatment of God's role in farming, human work is best understood as responsive engagement to the created order in which we find ourselves, with both that order and our own capacities being grounded in the same transcendent God. God, we might say, is more present to our work than we are to ourselves.

Lastly, getting clear on the nature of work in the garden—experienced as "spontaneous joy"—clarifies the effects of the fall. That is, examining the nature of work in Eden helps to clarify just how damaged by sin is our own experience of work. After the fall, Augustine writes, Adam "was sent away from the paradise of delight to work the earth from which he had been taken, that is, to toil in this body and there if he could to save up merit and earn the right to return" (*Gn. adv. Man.* 34). The fall, we know, changes everything about work. And so, it is to the nature of that fall and its effects that we must now turn.

3

The Effects of Sin on Work

For what will it profit them if they gain the whole world but forfeit their life? Or what will they give in return for their life?

MT. 16:26

The great question is whether human beings ought to regard themselves as things to be enjoyed, used, or both.

AUGUSTINE
DDC I.22

Introduction

As I established in Chapter 2, it is only after the fall that labor became difficult under divine curse. This is due, Augustine explains, to the transformation of the will in the fall. The task of this chapter is to elucidate (1) the effects of sin on our experience of work and (2) articulate an Augustinian strategy through which we can undertake cursed work faithfully. Put differently, this chapter will provide an answer to the question of how a Christian ought to work faithfully in a world of sin.

As such, I will examine Augustine's understanding of the fall in the next section. Adam and Eve's sin ushered in a new phase of human being. In the wake of that event, the whole of humanity entered into a state of sin as a form of divine punishment. Augustine believes that condition or state is passed onto each human being, such that we are born in a state of sin. And in that state, as we will show in time, we die, we experience pain, we see breakdowns in our natural environment, we get tired, we fight with disease, and we experience bodily disorder. Such a state of sin effects our work in that it makes created realities perishable, contingent. Hence the experience of toil in work.

In the wake of that cosmic analysis, I then turn to a brief examination of the nature of sinful action, with special attention being given to the nature and experience of work. For Augustine, humanity's entrance into sin entails the disordering of our minds and wills such that our loves are, when we are left to ourselves, out of order. In Augustine's read, ignorance (of the mind) and weakness (of the will) refer to a singular spiritual problem. That is, these two effects of sin work with one another to ensure that the individual acts out of self-interest (rather than love of God and neighbor) (Dodaro 2008, 29). Within such a state, ignorance and weakness ensure that one is simply incapable of acting virtuously in and of their own volition. And if self-interest underlies each sinful action, then the we can safely conclude that the real problem with most kinds of sin is the love animating our relation to the action or object in question; we love it out of self-interest. And so to follow Augustine's understanding of the effects of sin on work requires us to think about the relations and attachments that play out in our working lives: to our work, to those we work with, and to the products of our work. I then conclude the section with a brief overview of Augustine's understanding of the resolution to the problem of sin, which is centered around Christ's entrance into human being. We are saved in God's acceptance of the limitations of being a body in time and space (Williams 2016a, 11). And that taking on of human being makes possible a transformation in humans. That grace-funded transformation—stretched out across time—enables voluntary practices that reopen our minds to the love and goodness of God and the world (Mathewes 1999, 202).

The transformation of the Christian across time, enabled as it is by the grace of God and Christ's incarnation, has particular relevance for how we work in a sinful world. And so, in the third section of this chapter, I think with Augustine about the possibilities of faithful work in a sinful world. Augustine wants to navigate the sinful world faithfully, so to think with Augustine about the effects of sin on work also requires that we consider the possibilities for faithful work, particularly when our world so regularly fosters unhealthy attachments to our work, working identities, and the fruits of our labors.

In what is surely the most constructive element of the chapter, I develop an economic reading of Augustine's use/enjoyment framework at the end of that third section. That framework should serve as a means through which we can understand and undertake our work amid our own sinful context. Much like we are to use our neighbors for the enjoyment of God, thereby loving them properly and humanly, so too are we to "use" ourselves toward that gracious end in work. As Augustine notes, we "are ourselves also things" (*doc. Chr.* I.20). He thinks this is implied in Jesus' commandment to love our neighbor as ourselves. As such, we must use ourselves "for the sake of the one whom we are to enjoy." Every aspect of our persons—all agency, projects, and professional undertakings— "must be whisked along toward that point to which the whole impetus of [our] love is hastening." The self—and its work—can only be properly used, loved, and related to when placed in service of one's enjoyment of God.

But first, the fall.

Fall, Curse, Sinful Work, Redemption

Fall

Adam and Eve, prior to any act of sin, lacked for nothing good. Their love and attachment of God was direct and unimpeded, and they righteously obeyed God's instructions to tend to the garden and avoid eating from the tree of life. Augustine, believing in a literal Adam and Eve, argues that the fullness of humanity would have been brought into that unimpeded joy had Adam and Eve continued in their sinless ways for a longer period of time. At that point, he says, sin would have become impossible, and happiness would have been fully, finally secured.

While I have already articulated Augustine's view of the historicity of Eden (and my own), it must be stressed here that the historicity of the garden narrative is emphatically not what he is most interested in when reading about the fall. For Augustine, the narrative is less about the particular order of events in that lush garden than it is about the mysterious inner workings of the soul through which that first couple redirected their loves and turned away from God. But he also argues that an evil will necessarily preceded an evil action; the Devil's attempt to deceive Eve depended on some familiarity with evil. That is, the appeal and success of the temptation presuppose the desire for the prohibited fruit. The transformation preceded the temptation (*civ. Dei.* XIV.11). The basic characteristics of this primordial fall are applicable even if one doesn't believe in a literal Adam and Eve.

According to Augustine's theological system, Adam and Eve's Fall ushered the world into original sin. They succumbed to temptation willfully (rather than being coerced) because of their prideful attraction to the promise of being "like God" (Mann 2014, 106). In the wake of that event, humanity takes on a sinful condition as punishment, which he believes entails the loss of immortality, susceptibility to physical pain, the loss of a naturally perfect environment, fatigue, aging, disease, and bodily disorder (*civ. Dei.* XIV.16–19; Hill 2004, 11.32.42; Mann 2014, 106).

According to *De libero arbitrio*, Adam and Eve were rational and unwise (*lib. arb.* 3.18.52 – 3.25.77; Wetzel 2008, 79). That is, they had the intellectual capacity to recognize God's command as a command that ought to be obeyed, and yet they lacked the fortification against Satan's temptation and lies. Again, Augustine believes they would have attained wisdom had they persisted in their resistance to temptation, but they did not. Their giving into sin established the mortal chain that stretches into each new generation, and each subsequent moral agent inherits a fallen agency, which James Wetzel argues entails "a greater ignorance of where wisdom lies and a diminished capacity to act on what knowledge remains" (Wetzel 2008, 80). This inherited condition is innate to each descendent of humanity, by which he means each human being.

It is only after the fall that labor became difficult under divine curse. As Jeremy Kidwell notes, "[Augustine] conceives the implications of 'toil' broadly, arguing that the Fall affects human work by rendering created realities perishable (or 'contingent')" (Kidwell 2013, 779). Even if one manages to avoid the all-too-common exploitative practices of overpricing goods, false advertising, and bogus sales tactics, one's labor, even when ethically related to and carried out, is still regularly marked by frustration and resistance (*op. mon.* 13.14). Under such conditions, the very things we labor on inevitably enter into a state of decay the moment our activity ceases (Arbesmann 1973, 250 n. 6).

The fall thus has significant consequences on our experience of work by transforming the work itself. But the human will and intellect are transformed in the process as well, all of which have equally significant implications for our capacities for work, the way we relate to our work, and our understanding of that work. It is thus to the effect(s) of the fall on our will and intellect that we now turn in order to fully tease out the effects of sin on our work.

My Sin, My Work

As previously noted, interiority is a self-subverting reality (Turner 1995, 69). I always stand in relation to God, the world, and others, and my own understanding of myself necessarily depends on first turning toward God in love. Love thus plays a crucial role in the life of the human. Whatever the self is, it is determined and constituted in and through its loves.[1] When properly ordered, one's love of God

---

[1] I am patterning my use of "love" and "loves" after Eric Gregory's astute treatment. Gregory notes that Augustine primarily uses three terms for love: *amor*, *dilectio*, and *caritas*, even as he tended to use the terms interchangeably (much like he does with *mens*, *mens humana*, and *anima*). Like Gregory, I hereby follow Augustine's interchangeable use of those terms. And while Gregory uses the generic term for his project of developing an ethic of citizenship, I mainly use the term to characterize the human's specific modes of relationality and attachment (be they to the self, the things of the world, the world itself, other humans, or God), all of which follow a cluster of desires. For Augustine, all humans desire beatitude (i.e., happiness), even as our disordered desires and wills direct us to inordinately love things incapable of delivering such happiness. In fact, the defining distinction between Augustine's moral psychology and that of the Stoics and the Manichees was that Augustine maintained the possibility (at least in the latter half of his career) of a will divided against itself. That is, as James Wetzel notes in *Augustine and the Limits of Virtue*, "It is the same soul (*eadem anima*), divided in its will, that stands torn between two objects of desire, two perceived goods" (130). Augustine did not believe that grace re-makes one's desires in any sort of immediate or total sense before death; even in the midst of a life of grace, we are still capable of desiring the wrong things, all the while recognizing God as the singular source of goodness capable of satisfying our desire

should situate and direct one's love toward others, the self, and the world at large. That is, in our love of God, we come to love others and the world most appropriately. For Augustine, we are to love the world precisely because God loves it, and we come to love the world by participating in God's love of the world and being fully in the world (Mathewes 2008, 84).

That vision, Augustine insists, was disrupted in the fall, though. The entrance into sin entails the disordering of our minds and wills such that our loves are, when we are left to ourselves, out of order. The real problem with most kinds of sin is the love that animates our relation to the action or object in question. That is, sin, for Augustine, is "more dispositional than metaphysical" (Mathewes 2008, 89–90). We are supposed to love the world in God, but we tend to love it for ourselves apart from God. And in so doing, Augustine insists, we tend to overestimate what the world can deliver to us. The fundamental problem with us as sinful people is precisely that we love the world too much, that we hope for the things and activities of the world to deliver something to us that they simply cannot—happiness.

Even our attempts to return to a love of the world ordered according to our love for God are foiled by our continued desires to love the wrong things inordinately. Augustine notes time and again that the mind, as well as its capacity for intelligence and knowledge, is limited and disordered in the state of sin to the extent that the sinful person "is unable not only to cling to and enjoy God but even to endure God's immutable light" (*civ. Dei* XI.2). Ethical action thus stems from a properly integrated self, whereas wicked actions stem from disintegration. Our repetitive decisions to love the wrong things, or to love things in the wrong way, are doomed to failure. Created entities simply cannot deliver happiness. We are certainly free to choose, Augustine argues, but our internal disintegration (our misdirected loves) has enslaved the will to the extent that we simply cannot will or love anything properly of our own accord. The will

---

for happiness. Within such a state, "love" refers to the modes of relationality we undertake. As such, our loves are properly directed when they follow and actualize our properly ordered desires, and our loves are misdirected when they follow and actualize improper modes of desire (Mathewes 1999, 202; Gregory 2010, 35 n.7; Wetzel 2008, 130).

directs one according to its loves and desires, and, in the midst of a sinful state, our wills and loves are misdirected to the extent that we continually prohibit our own flourishing (Mathewes 1999, 206). In such a state, we are unable to follow our wills wholeheartedly. Our previous actions have formed a "chain of habit" to which we are shackled (*conf.* 8.5.10; P. Brown 2013, 166).

Again, humanity's entrance into sin entails the disordering of our minds and wills such that our loves are, when we are left to ourselves, out of order. Augustine argues that the ignorance that stems from sin prevents one from understanding their soul in relation God as the source of goodness and beauty, and all of this prevents any coherent understanding of self-motivation. Such ignorance also prevents one from reaching any clear conception of the requirements for acting justly in a given set of circumstances. Weakness, on the other hand, refers to the self's inability to act justly (Dodaro 2008, 28). Ignorance and weakness, which map onto the intellect and will, refer to a singular spiritual problem—these two effects of sin interact with each other and contribute to the same outcome of self-interest before God and others (Dodaro 2008, 29). Within such a state, ignorance and weakness ensure that one is simply incapable of acting virtuously in and of their own volition.

To follow Augustine's treatment of sin under the guise of a larger investigation of the nature and limits of work requires we think about relations and attachment: attachment to our work, those we work with, and the products of our work. Those relations and attachments are quite frequently sinful.

For example, as I noted in the introduction, Americans have a problematic attachment (i.e., sinful relation) to their work. We are, simply put, obsessed. We not only work more and more obsessively than other developed countries, but we also position work as the cornerstone of our adult selves and moral lives. Whether it is because of a certain emptiness lying at the heart of one's sense of self, an inability to rest, the need to perpetually accrue a sense of increased security, or something else entirely, when we structure our lives around our work, we ask our work to deliver something to us that it simply cannot: happiness. And to position work as the center of our selves is to attempt to displace (or perhaps foreclose our awareness of) the divine otherness truly operative as the ground of our being.

But sinful attachment is far from an individual affair in Augustine's mind. It is, of course, always relational, and the relations refer to people as often as they do objects or actions. And our working relations are often quite sinful too. When our work exploits or harms those we are in relation to by way of the work, we are working sinfully. That is, if my compensation and role depends on an exploitative relation to my coworker, my work depends on a sinful relationship. Whether it be asking them to do unjust things, fostering unhealthy habits in them (perhaps by way of the work culture and norms I help create), or unjustly paying them, the damaged relationship impacts the whole of my work and my attachment to it.

Redemption

The resolution to such a dilemma is not that we stop loving the world altogether. Quite the opposite, in fact. As Mathewes notes, "The world is not ultimately the problem; we are" (Mathewes 2008, 90). Rather, when sin is rendered in this way, redemption must entail a change in the ways we love. And this is precisely what stereotypical renderings of Augustine's anxieties (and Plato's, for that matter) regarding sexuality, bodies, and materiality entirely miss. Augustine does not want us to stop loving bodies in order to love God; loving God, he thinks, should transform our loves so that we begin to love them in God and, therefore, to love them humanly. This transformation leads our desires and will back to their natural desires.

Such a transformation is only brought about, Augustine argues, by Christ's entrance into human being. We are saved in God's acceptance of the limitations of being a body in time and space (Williams 2016a, 11). Christ's presence, he thinks, is itself a declaration of God's ongoing attention to us, which is constitutive of our own identities. The incarnation of the Word in Jesus transforms us in and through a series of historical events, and it thereby declares that God's attention is in touch with those aspects of our lives that remain beyond even our own comprehension (Williams 2016a, 12). That transformation—stretched out across time—is funded through the grace of Christ, which enables voluntary practices that reopen our minds to the love and goodness of God and the world

(Mathewes 1999, 202). This, Augustine would say, echoing Paul, is simply what it means to "put on Christ." It is in Christ's unification with flesh that our loves can be redeemed, but that transformation first requires coming to terms with our own natures as they are constituted by those same conditions of time, space, material, and so on (*conf.* VII.18.24). Asking who or what I am must always be asked in relation to the narrative of Christ's taking on of finitude.

The transformation of the Christian across time, enabled as it is by the grace of God and Christ's incarnation, has particular relevance for how we work in a sinful world. As I noted in Chapter 1, Augustine regularly turned to Romans 7 in order to speak of the tension Christians experience in the time between their redemption in Jesus and the resurrection of the dead. We remain stuck between two persuasive masters pulling us in opposite directions. Hence Paul's confusion regarding his own actions: he does what he does not want to do, and even his desire to act in accordance with the good of Christ is overcome by his seemingly equally alluring desire for misdeeds. Being under grace, on this side of the incarnation of Christ, does not end our sinful desires. It does, however, mean that we have been given the grace through which (by the power of the Spirit) we can overcome those sinful desires. Put differently, the world and the creatures in it are being redeemed, but the process is not yet complete. And the task of Christian ethics is to determine how we ought to undertake action and thought in ways that are marked by the transformation made possible by Christ, particularly within the context of a fallen world and our ongoing sinful desires. Put more simply: the ethical task at hand is to determine how what faithful work looks like within a world of sin. What does putting on Christ, acquiring virtue, and conforming ourselves to God look like as it pertains to working within in a sinful world? It is to this question we now turn.

Working Faithfully in a World of Sin (or "Using Myself Now")

Augustine wants to navigate the sinful world faithfully, so to think with Augustine about the effects of sin on work also requires that we consider the possibilities for faithful work, particularly when our world so regularly fosters unhealthy attachments to our work, working identities, and the fruits of our labors.

Even still, during our time in the world, labor features (at least when it is properly related to, directed, undertaken, and contextualized) the same kind of opportunity for moral reformation found in any other form of worldly suffering (*civ. Dei.* 18.49). Such an opportunity exists, for Augustine, precisely because labor cannot be totally reduced to earthly, material conditions. He encourages his readers to undertake their spiritual formation with the same sort of discipline, vision, and agency that animates daily labor: "the way is narrow, attended by work and suffering" (*op. mon.* 29.37).

Augustine does not, however, simply prioritize spiritual and mental labor over against manual labor. As he explains, manual labor undertaken at the expense of mental labor is not wholesome, and mental labor carried out at the expense of physical labor is said to be negligent (*S.* 37.5–6). He thus highlights a crucial connection between labor and the broader practice of spiritual formation. This is precisely why, in Kidwell's analysis, the category of resurrection is never far from his treatment of labor or its contingent nature. There is, he argues, a crucial, if limited, line of continuity that runs from the original goodness of the created order (labor included) and the present world that awaits God's coming judgment and redemption. "As a result," Kidwell writes, "[Augustine] sees the curse of toil as having a redemptive function: it improves us and draws us nearer to God, offering a foretaste of our coming resurrection" (Kidwell 2013, 779).

That is, bodily labor, when properly ordered and directed, should facilitate the kind of unending spiritual growth Augustine thinks should mark the life of a Christian's journey into God (*Trin.* 14). When navigated in this manner, one's labor becomes an extension—a modality or unique expression—of one's prayer life. Augustine's use/enjoyment framework, I am arguing here, has profound implications for the ways we undertake our work amid such a context.

Use and Enjoyment

Augustine's *De Doctrina Christiana* is a treatise on Christian teaching wherein Augustine sets out to analyze the mechanics through which one might understand strange, alien texts. Most particularly, though, it is a series of sustained reflections on the relationship between *signum* and *res*—signs and things (Williams 2016d, 41). We encounter myriad *res* in the world, some of which signify something beyond themselves while others do not. In the world, *res* operate in conjunction with our wills in distinct ways: they can be either used or enjoyed. We find, in our time in the world, things meant to be "enjoyed," things meant to be "used," and things which do the "enjoy-ing" while being "used." According to Augustine, we properly "enjoy" something when it delights us—to the highest degree—apart from any external referent or additional end (*civ. Dei.* XI.25). It is the very nature of that object that sustains enjoyment and happiness. Augustine writes, "Our final good is that for the sake of which other things are to be directed, while it is itself to be desired for its own sake" (*civ. Dei.* XIX.1). "Enjoyment" thus consists in "clinging to something lovingly for its own sake," whereas "use" consists in a relation that refers one toward what is to be "enjoyed" (*doc. Chr.* I.3.3). In light of this schema, there is a crucial connection between our own (universal) desire for happiness and the ways in which we relate to the things and people we find in the world (*conf.* X.23.33).

Such happiness, though, is not so easy to come by; it is not readily available to us in those things we encounter in the world (*conf.* X.21.30). According to Augustine, God is not determined by anything outside itself, and God requires no superfluous interpretation to be what God is (*doc. Chr.* I.5.5). God is thus supremely and uniquely *res*—a thing learned through signs whose being is not determined in and through the use or meaning of anything else (*doc. Chr.* I.2.2). No sign, therefore, can properly represent or live up to the reality that is this *res* (apart from the *signum* this *res* willingly becomes in the incarnation) (Williams 2016d, 43). So, for Augustine, everything is *signum* in light of God being *res*. We can only find our happiness in that thing capable of sustaining "enjoyment" (i.e., God alone), and we are to "use" the things of the world on our way toward the happiness that "enjoyment" makes possible (*doc. Chr.* I.3.3). Augustine speaks of the "use" of such things as "crutches and props for reaching the things that will make us happy, and enabling us to keep them" (*doc. Chr.* I.3.3). Within such a perspective, we are to "proceed from temporal and bodily things to grasp those that are eternal and spiritual" (*doc. Chr.* I.4.4). The distinction only makes sense when the ultimate end of loving and knowing God is understood and prioritized.

God, in God's triune, supreme, uniquely-*res* nature, is what humans are to enjoy because God is the ultimate source of happiness. Only that which "constitutes the life of bliss" is capable of being enjoyed. God is to be enjoyed, Augustine argues, precisely because God is eternal and unchanging (*doc. Chr.* I.22.20). As he writes in *The Confessions,* "When I seek you, my God, what I am seeking is a life of happiness. Let me seek you that my soul may live, for as my body draws its life from my soul, so does my soul draw its life from you" (*conf.* X.20.29). God, as the source of our very selves, should be the object of focus and the end toward which we direct ourselves (*doc. Chr.* I.20.21). There is, in fact, nothing else capable of sustaining such happiness:

> This is the happy life, and this alone: to rejoice in you, about you, and because of you. This is the life of happiness, and it is not to be found anywhere else. Whoever thinks there can be some other is chasing a joy that is not the true one; yet such a person's will has not turned away from all notion of joy. (*conf.* X.22.32)

To "enjoy" God, in whose triune image we are made, is to move into the fullness of happiness (*Trin.* I.8.18).

Aiming at such enjoyment of God is necessarily a totalizing endeavor. Pursuing the "enjoyment" of God entails the totality of one's life given that there is no surplus category of my person or being which is not to be directed toward that enjoyment (*doc. Chr.* I.20.21). And given that Augustine understands the person as a union of body and soul living in the material order, pursuing that "enjoyment" requires a particular mode of navigating bodily life. The question for Augustine becomes how one is to properly be in the world so as to facilitate such "enjoyment." It is this primary relation of person to God that is supposed to structure and direct all other forms of relationality. We "use" something, he explains, when "we seek it for the sake of some further end" (*civ. Dei.* XI.25). For Augustine, we properly relate to the things of the world—that is, all that is not God—when we "use" them in our pursuit of "enjoyment" of God. Work, I will argue, is no exception.

Improper and Proper Use

Such a framework places a heavy emphasis on the ways we relate to the things of the world. Augustine insists, time and again, that the things of the world are good presicely because they exist as God's creation. But to "use" something is to love it properly, in light of its place within that order of creation. One example Augustine gives is that of food: a wise person can make proper "use" of the most decadent, expensive food without slipping into greediness or self-indulgence, while a fool can feast in gluttony in relation to something simple like chocolate snack cakes (*doc. Chr.* III.12.19). The moral status of the act of eating therefore depends less on the content of the food itself than it does on my relation to the food. He writes, "For in all matters of this kind it is not the nature of the things we make use of, but our reason for making use of them and the manner in which we set about getting them, that decides whether what we do deserves approval or disapproval" (*doc. Chr.* III.12.19). All things are indeed lawful. The key is our relation to the object or act in question and a right will gives way to a proper form of love (*doc. Chr.* III.12.18; *civ. Dei.* XIV.7). Or, perhaps most simply, one makes good "use" of the things of the world when one relates to them in order to "enjoy" God rather than in an attempt at some form of "enjoyment" of the world itself (*civ. Dei.* XV.7).

When we "enjoy" what is to be "used," though, we disrupt our own progression into the life of God; such an act is nothing but the directing of our love toward the wrong end (*doc. Chr.* I.3.3; *civ. Dei.* XIV.7). Augustine writes, "For anyone who loves something else along with you, but does not love it for your sake, loves you less" (*conf.* X.29.40). The key to improper "use" is that it inevitably leads to disappointment because it is most commonly based on an overestimation of the thing's potential (*doc. Chr.* I.38.42). The issue Augustine points to is not some depraved, evil creation that must be jettisoned to get to higher, more pure realities. Things are good simply by drawing their existence from God. How could they be otherwise, he wonders? God, after all, made things exceedingly good (*conf.* X.34.51). The problem, rather, is that people "are more immediately engrossed in other things which more surely make them miserable than that other reality, so faintly remembered, can make them happy" (*conf.* X.23.33). In sticking with the example of food, it makes good sense, then, that in speaking of David's temptation with water in 2 Samuel 23 and Christ's temptation to convert stones into bread in the wilderness Augustine explains that the sin rests not in the desire for meat or bread, but in the form of hunger that gave rise to anger at God. The problem emerges in a lustful relation to the food rather than in the food itself (*conf.* X.31.46).

Perhaps the best example of improper use is Augustine's own telling of his relation to the unknown friend of Book IV of the *Confessions*. It is there that Augustine analyzes his past experience of mourning and dread in the wake of a close friend's death. As he recollects, he was so upset at his friend's death that he found himself hating the places he had come to associate with his deceased friend— those places were now incapable of facilitating the friend's presence and proximity (*conf.* IV.4.9). Augustine finds himself swinging back and forth between wanting to die himself and being overcome with the fear of death given that his own death necessarily features the end of his memory of that friend. The most interesting aspect of this retrospective telling, though, is that, over time, Augustine realizes the ways in which this series of responses represents his own failure to love his friend humanly (*conf.* IV.7.12). He had failed to take the finitude of that other creature to heart, somehow (perhaps even subconsciously) hoping that this other human could transcend its mortal nature and thereby provide the sort of happiness all mortal things search for (Williams 2016a, 5). To love in lust is to love something on its own account, devoid of its place within the order of things. It is therefore to overestimate what that thing can deliver. Such a form of love is corrosive precisely because it fosters an illicit form of "enjoyment" aimed at the wrong object (*Trin.* IX.2.13).

In contrast to this overestimation of a friend's nature and capacities, Augustine explains that we are to love other people in relation to our love of God. That is, we do not love others as the ultimate horizon—we are not to "enjoy" them in themselves as much as we are to "use" them in the "enjoyment" of God. As such, we are to love each other for the sake of something else (*doc. Chr.* I.22.20). Properly "using" another, though, entails "enjoying" God in that person (*doc. Chr.* I.33.37). In this sense, loving a person for God's sake does not prohibit loving them for their (and my own) sake as well. Rather, whenever I manage to love my neighbor for God's sake, I inevitably love that neighbor according to their best interest (as well as my own) precisely because I am loving them and "enjoying" them in God, where we properly belong together (*doc. Chr.* I.22.21 n. 22).[2] To properly "use" something or someone is to let our love of that object refer our delights to our final goal in God (*doc. Chr.* I.22.20; I.33.36) Proper "use," in this sense, depends on properly ordered love. One must be able to properly evaluate things and then love them in the right order "so that you do not love what is not to be loved, or fail to love what is to be loved, or have a greater love for what should be loved less, or an equal love for things that should be loved less or more, or a lesser or greater love for things that should be loved equally" (*doc. Chr.* I.27.28). The point is not that creatures and the things of the world cannot or should not be loved, but that proper love of the creature in service of one's love of God leads to a shift from covetousness and lust to charity (*Trin.* IX.2.13).

An Economic Reading of Use/Enjoyment

The use/enjoyment framework, when read in an economic register, treats all questions of value and relation in relation to God, who is itself the highest form and source of all value and goodness. God is the very ground from which all goodness and beauty arise, and God is therefore the standard according to which all other things are properly valued. Said differently, God is to be enjoyed, and all other things are to be used. The use/enjoyment framework provides us with a conceptual rubric through which we can evaluate and determine the justice (or lack thereof) of any number of economic systems, proposals, and practices. Any sketch of the systematic organization of the production, distribution, and consumption of

---

[2] As Edmund Hill notes in his edition of Augustine's *De Trinitate*, Augustine insists in *De Doctrina Christiana* that "we must love ourselves and other men, *non propter se, sed propter aliud*, not for our own sake, but for God's sake. This is not properly speaking, according to his own definition, to enjoy ourselves and others, though it can also be called enjoying ourselves and others in God; it can be called using and loving, using because we thus refer ourselves and others to the supreme good, loving because we value ourselves in ourselves, but not however purely for ourselves. This, he is careful to point out, does not dishonor ourselves or others but simply treats human beings according to their deepest ontology as creatures, that is, as beings with a built-in reference or orientation on their creator (1,22,21)." See Augustine's *De Trinitate* IX.2.13 n. 24; 349.

goods must ascribe to the standards of just relations articulated in the framework in order to qualify for "use" rather than "abuse." Money, debt, property, and work are things and practices to be used in service of a shared enjoyment of God. Any approach to those economic entities and practices that fails to foster such a mode of relation is both unjust and abusive, and therefore becomes condemnable from an Augustinian perspective.

It is important to emphasize the differences between my reading of Augustine's framework and Kant's articulation of means and ends. A Kantian "means to an end" is not the issue here. Augustine's terminology of use/enjoyment is much more aimed at recognizing that any earthly, creaturely good (good as it might be) is ultimately for the purpose of directing one toward their highest end in God. Proper use of the earth and its plants, animals, and other humans should be in service of our knowing God, which is emphatically not a manipulative, dominating phenomenon for Augustine. As Charles Mathewes helpfully points out, the earth is distinctly not "mine to be consumed" within this framework. Proper use would likely therefore entail less "usage" (as we commonly hear that term now) given that all aspects of one's life need to be in service of humanity's highest calling of knowing and loving God rather than satisfying my own corrupted desires and aims. The use-model, then, is not Kantian; it is not just about using things as means. Rather, it is a proscription against ascribing too much hope to any one cluster of things, hoping them to be the God they most certainly cannot be. Augustine is thus greatly concerned with our tendency to instrumentalize our neighbors and the world itself, to use them for our own purposes and egoist drives. His prescription of use actually reads much like Kant's proscription—Augustine urges us to "use" the goods of this world in order to avoid manipulating them for our own misdirected interests or expecting that they can provide us with any sort of lasting happiness (Mathewes 2008, 86). We properly use such goods when we receive them as the good gifts from God that they are, treating them with the respect, dignity, and alterity they deserve.

Such an economic reading of the use/enjoyment framework has profound implications for our contemporary understandings and practices of work—what I am calling "the use of the self." Much like we are to use our neighbors for the enjoyment of God, thereby loving them properly and humanly, so too are we to "use" ourselves toward that gracious end. As Augustine notes, we "are ourselves also things" (*doc. Chr.* I.22.20). He thinks this is implied in Jesus' commandment to love our neighbor as ourselves (*doc. Chr.* I.26.27). As such, we must use ourselves "for the sake of the one whom we are to enjoy." Every aspect of our persons—all agency, projects, and professional undertakings—"must be whisked along toward that point to which the whole impetus of [our] love is hastening" (*doc. Chr.* I.22.21). The task is therefore to learn how to properly "use" and thereby love ourselves in order to properly benefit from and relate our own work in relation to each other and in service of our highest callings.

Augustine actually speaks of such modes of work on multiple occasions (one of which I analyze, in-depth, in the next chapter). He touches on the topic, in a passing way, in the tenth book of *The Confessions* when he notes that even the best of work will not suffice if it is not undertaken in service of and relation to one's enjoyment of God. Craftpersons with creativity, ingenuity, and meticulous skill, he explains, create clothing, household goods, and tools whose value and beauty vastly exceed their intended purposes and uses. They create at a remarkably high level of quality, but they misuse their own agencies whenever they undertake their work in a way that forsakes "the One within by whom they were made, and so destroy what they were made to be by driving it out of doors" (*conf.* X.34.53). Such an insight makes good sense when received in light of Augustine's doctrine of transcendence. Whatever beauty emerges in human design or blueprints ultimately stems from God, and the ultimate meaning (as well as the norms by which we ought to relate to that mode of agency or the objects/fruits of our labor) of that work is not readily available in the act of working itself. Work must find its place in the order of things; it too must be "used" in service of "enjoying" God.

This approach frees us from the need to cling to our own work as though our final end, happiness, or value were somehow bound up in that context. We are thereby freed to refuse the ways we so regularly abuse ourselves in and through our work. Any "use" of the body and its agency that does not frame its activities in conjunction with humanity's end is misdirected. This does not, however, denigrate other forms of human agency and activity as much as it speaks of the end toward which they are to be directed. It becomes clear that capitalism (or any other economic system, for that matter) cannot possibly deliver a proper vision of agency or work because the final end toward which all human agency is directed (i.e., God—that being both present and absent from which any definitive meaning for the self must stem) remains beyond its purview. The self—and its work—can only be properly used, loved, and related to when placed in service of one's enjoyment of God. Faithful work must be undertaken in worship of God.

Much like we are to use our neighbors for the enjoyment of God, thereby loving them properly and humanly, so too are we to "use" ourselves toward that gracious end in work. As such, we must use ourselves "for the sake of the one whom we are to enjoy." Every aspect of our persons—all agency, projects, and professional undertakings—"must be whisked along toward that point to which the whole impetus of [our] love is hastening" (*doc. Chr.* I.22.21). The self—and its work —can only be properly used, loved, and related to when placed in service of one's enjoyment of God.

Conclusion

Phrasing work in terms of the capacities of the soul is helpful because it clarifies the ways our sinful agency and a sinful world impact our experience of work. The soul (and its capacities) I described above simply is the structure that is, for Augustine, disordered in the wake of sin to the extent that it has been turned inside out and therefore stands in need of redemption (Hill 2012, 325). In sin, the psyche's highest functioning is disrupted by way of a consent to the lower, *sciential* functions in a lust for power, which leads one into the depths of carnal enslavement. The disorientation of the soul and the impairment of the divine image in the *psyche* are thus caused by a turning away from God for the sake of self-love. In prioritizing private possession over and above common participation, one enters into a state of sin, which is certainly not without its subversive economic implications (Hill 2012, 327). As Hill notes, "It is only when the *sciential* function has consented to this divine condescension by *faith*, and begun to control the appetites of the outer man by *virtue*, that the highest *sapiential* function can begin to be released once more for the loving contemplation of the divine" (Hill 2012, 328).

Our animal life necessitates some form of work, and yet in sin we remain both (1) ignorant of the good toward which we should direct that work and (2) incapable of actually willing our work toward that end. Our economies and cultures have commodified and economized our work since the agricultural revolution, which has entwined our livelihoods, potential for flourishing, and basic sense of self with larger economic forces, pressures, norms, and demands. Amid these swirling pressures and demands, Augustine nonetheless insists that the activity itself be directed toward the human's final end—God.

The task, then, is learning how to properly "use" and thereby love ourselves in order to direct our labor in service of others and our higher callings. This, I have no established, is what it means to work faithfully in a world of sin. The ethical standard is clear enough, but the mechanics by which that standard is met must be sketched next.

The good news for this investigation is that Augustine wrote extensively on the role of work in the monastic context in *Op. mon.* While he does not offer a unified, systematic theory of labor in that text, such a theory can be assembled when read in conjunction with the use/enjoyment dyad (and the previously stated economic implications). And the theoretical system undergirding those insights can and should help us deploy Augustine's insights into our own economic situation, drastically different from Augustine's as it might be. It is to that peculiar little text we must turn our attention toward next.

4

Working in the *Saeculum*

It is the love of truth, then, that seeks holy leisure, and it is the drive of love that takes on righteous activity.

AUGUSTINE
DCD XIX.19

What should be the disposition of a citizen of that eternal City, the heavenly Jerusalem, except that he should hold in common with his brother whatever he gains with his own labor and that he should receive whatever he needs from the common supply, saying with him whose precept and example he has followed: "As having nothing yet possessing all things."

AUGUSTINE
DCD XIX.19

Introduction

Augustine offers us some concrete examples of the ways in which we can properly use ourselves for the enjoyment of God. Augutsine insisted throughout his theological oeuvre tht labor has both dignity and value, even within a sinful world. Augustine manages to affirm the dignity of labor without universalizing it, mandating it, or even denigrating life outside of labor time. One's moral duty to labor, Augustine argues (along with the vast majority of the class of Roman cultural elites to which he belonged), is actually a subset of one's broader civic duties, and it is a necessary component of the social fabric in our fallen world. From within such a framework, the moral and spiritual task of faithful work is to properly use oneself for the sake of enjoying God, which necessarily entails properly loving my self, my limits, my God, and my neighbor in and through my working experience.

This chapter aims to accomplish three things: (1) develop a brief treatment of an under-analyzed Augustinian text, *De Opere Monachorum* (*op. mon.*) and situate that text's labor-related insights in relation to Augustine's other commentary regarding the nature and function of labor; (2) theorize the possibility (and effects) of one's labor being transformed into a modality of one's life of prayer; and (3) describe the difference this kind of graced, virtuous labor can make in the lives of laborers today.

In short, I will argue that Augustine's treatment of monastic labor provides insights into how one ought to relate to one's labor within a world dominated by global capitalism. By grounding labor within a life of liturgy and virtue, labor's meaning and form are altogether transformed. When undertaken in virtue, such grace-enabled labor has the ability to sharpen one's love of God, preparing the self for further transformation into the life of God.

I begin with a brief analysis of *op. mon.* in order to argue that labor can play a crucial role in one's temporal progression toward the beatific vision when properly related to, directed, undertaken, and contextualized. This is true in spite of the emphatically noncentral role labor plays in Augustine's theological anthropology (not to mention the fact that, in the wake of the fall, we experience labor in its cursed condition, even if Augustine believes Adam and Eve certainly labored prior to that fall). The context and manner in which labor is undertaken makes all the difference, and that difference is only ever actualized through the transformative power of grace.

As I will show there, Augustine understood the rule and liturgy to coincide not with a list of individual acts, but with the expression of an entire life. When undertaken in this manner, labor becomes but one element of a larger life of liturgy and prayer. Similar to Pierre Hadot's distinction between philosophical discourse and the philosophical life—a series of existential commitments that structured the entirety of one's being in the world, of which philosophical discourse was a crucial but singular part—the context of the labor situates the activity within a larger form of being or way of living (Hadot 2002, 3). Under such conditions, it is possible for labor to become a modality of prayer such that the whole of one's labor is grafted into one's larger life of prayer before God.

After analyzing *op. mon.*, I identify some practical implications for non-monastic labor within Augustine's proposals. The theological virtues of faith, hope, and love are intrinsic to the life of the believer and provide something of a structure and framework of Christian existence. Rendered this way, the virtues become one mode of response to God's efficacious gift of transformative grace. In our lives in the world, we humans are being prepared for—made worthy of—what is to come in the new creation.

Such a transformation makes possible alternative modes of being and doing in the world, even to the extent that basic activities such as labor can be redirected toward the love of God and others. This transformed labor, which I refer to as "liturgical labor," features new understandings of time, relationality, and selfhood, all of which should make a concrete difference in the way we work in the contemporary world, marked as it is by global capitalism

De Opere Monachorum

Augustine's analysis of labor offers us some crucial insights about the nature and function of labor within a Christian theological framework, and those insights need not be confined to the context of the monastery alone. Augustine identifies in Paul a form of labor he thinks the monks are capable of enacting. Put differently, Augustine offers us some latent resources through which we might begin to properly order our loves in labor, even as we inhabit a labor culture that is profoundly disordered and therefore regularly commodifies, fetishizes, and overestimates labor. The goal of this section is to draw on Augustine's most sustained treatment in *op. mon.* in order to articulate the underlying vision of labor.

At the request of Aurelis (the Bishop of Carthage at the time), Augustine wrote *op. mon.* sometime around the year 400 in order to settle an ongoing dispute over monastic discipline (Grote 2013, 36 n. 6). A faction of monks was refusing to labor and trusting in alternative provisions based on a particular reading of Mt. 6:25-34.

The monks had undertaken a spiritually motivated, hermeneutically grounded labor strike. The strike was significant in the life of the monastery both because of the role labor played in the liturgy of the hours and the basic, necessary tasks required to cultivate a shared life in that monastic context.

Augustine begins his text by considering the argument of the monks. Citing Christ's parable of the birds that neither toil nor spin, these monks explained that they were refusing any manual labor in order to enable and prioritize a life exclusively dedicated to spiritual activities—prayer, reading, and meditation. The striking monks stood strong in the face of 2 Thess. 3:10 ("whoever will not work should not eat"); as we see in Augustine's text, those monks did not think Paul was referring to bodily labor in that passage. Rather, they argued that Paul exclusively referred to spiritual labor, which was the very form they were aiming to prioritize. Further, the monks argued that Paul could not possibly contradict Christ himself, who, in the Gospel of Matthew, urges his followers not to worry about what they will eat or wear. Christ seems to indicate that God will provide, even apart from one's own toil, so how could Paul possibly require the precise thing Christ frees believers from? (*op. mon.* 1.2). The only logical possibility, they argued, was that Paul was referring to spiritual labor. To substantiate this claim, the monks pointed to 1 Corinthians 3, wherein Paul speaks of Christian formation in terms of labor. In so doing, they identified a hermeneutical precedent. The monks were trying to avoid becoming the laborer who wastes their talent by burying it, and in the face of such concern, they faithfully tended to their spiritual labor. They read, prayed, and worshiped with the other brethren. They sought to comfort and encourage those who came to them weary from the toils of the world, and they had thrown off all physical labor in order to expand their capacities for such spiritual care. In so doing, Augustine makes clear, they assumed themselves to be operating in accordance with both the Gospel and apostolic precepts.

After briefly overviewing the striking monks' argument, Augustine shifts to criticism. Much of the problem, he argues, stems from their poor, self-oriented interpretation of Scripture (*op. mon.* 2.3). They were reading Paul's rejection of labor in an allegorical sense and the Matthean text literally, but Augustine argues they should do the precise opposite on both counts (Barsella 2014, 67). Can they not decipher that Christ is speaking in parables while Paul literally references physical labor? In order to rebut the monks' argument and practice, Augustine points to Paul's refusal of the right not to labor in order to help make sense of the Matthew passage in a different way. Paul, Augustine argues, has given the monks both a precept (in 2 Thess. 3:7-12) and his example in order to aid their understanding of labor. Augustine hopes to demonstrate that Paul wants Christians to take up manual labor, which he thinks can lead to great spiritual reward, in a way that enables them to provide the necessities of life for both themselves and others in need without becoming a burden to those around them (*op. mon.* 3.4). This is the basic thrust of Augustine's message to the monks.

In addition to helping the striking monks understand Paul's vision and urging them to follow his example, Augustine hopes to demonstrate that the Pauline passages the strikers are drawing on do not, in fact, contradict Christ's message in the Gospels. Paul's exemption from manual labor—an exemption, Augustine repeatedly reminds his readers, he neglected to claim—stemmed from his status as an apostle (*op. mon.* 4.5). Such an exemption, Augustine explains, was a legitimate apostolic practice. Apostles often did not engage in the manual labor required to provide themselves with the necessities of life, and they therefore accepted the gifts of nourishment from the people they were spiritually nourishing. Paul, however, refused to live on such alms for the good of the communities he was ministering to. In Augustine's reading of the narrative, Paul did not want to be an undue burden, even though his authority granted him the right to do so (*op. mon.* 7.8). Further, Paul hoped to avoid any suggestion that the Gospel was up for sale. It is Paul's insistence on laboring so as to not take advantage of the communities he was ministering to that so interests our author (*op. mon.* 13.14). Living off of the gifts of the communities to whom he was preaching, he worried, might suggest he was exchanging the good news of Christ's incarnation and resurrection for some bread, wine, and a warm bed (*op. mon.* 10.11).

Augustine certainly seems interested in highlighting the sheer audacity of the striking monks. If Paul himself, who had the legitimate right to throw off labor and claim alms, refused to do so, what makes the monks think they are so worthy of such a claim? Augustine remains similarly fascinated by the monks' increased free time. What, he wonders on multiple occasions, could they possibly be doing with their extra leisure time that is so drastically important? (*op. mon.* 17.20). Against their self-oriented mode of interpretation, Augustine insists that a proper reading of these texts demonstrates that "the Apostle performed manual work; that he provided his physical sustenance by means of that work; and that he did not avail himself of the right which the Lord had given to the Apostles, namely, that the preacher of the Gospel should live from the Gospel." And the import of this approach lies not in the sort of labor that Paul did; Augustine writes, "[w]hatever work men perform without guilt and trickery is good" (*op. mon.* 13.14).

It is worth noting that in building his basic argument that the monks should be laboring, Augustine avoids slipping into a trite reading of Paul's instruction to labor. Paul's intention (and Augustine's for that matter) is not to shame those incapable of laboring in this particular manner. In fact, he is quite comfortable with the shift from manual labor to administrative labor under such circumstances (Brockwell 1977, 99). Rather, Augustine points to Galatians 6 to highlight Paul's instruction to communities to provide preachers with the supplies they need for living, and he thus insists, along with Paul, that the goodness of one's labor rests, at least partially, in the ability to provide for the needs of the community. Augustine suggests that such a communal approach to labor and provision actually opens up a new relationship to labor itself. When freed from the love of and drive toward private possessions and accumulation, one is able to suffer with the lowly in solidarity, taking on their struggles and laboring to provide for those in need (*op. mon.* 16.19). Therein lies the shift from lust to charity (*Trin* 9.13).

Augustine is suggesting to the monks that the same basic activity they associate with greed and distraction from spiritual matters can be redeployed toward different, just ends when approached within the context of a community marked by the Gospel of Jesus Christ. But this is precisely the sort of potential and understanding that the monks' strict dualism prohibits. Those striking monks had erected a strict divide between their inner (spiritual) and outer (animal) needs, and they were aiming to address the former at the expense of the latter (*Trin.* 9–14). But this approach overlooks the composite relation of the soul to the body. We simply are not the sorts of creatures that can or should attend to spiritual needs alone; spiritual realities cannot be fostered apart from a proper navigation of our bodily lives. As Augustine argues, the realities of our bodily life dictate that we attend to the labor required to tend to ourselves. Whatever knowledge and love of God that the soul makes possible depends on the health and well-being of one's bodily life. So why do these striking monks assume that attending to their outer (animal) needs via labor has nothing to do with their spiritual formation? We can, he argues, labor in ways that enable our spiritual formation. This is why Augustine urges the monks to sing canticles while they labor: if they are so interested in praying and worshipping, they should take up those activities in the midst of their labor. Such an approach might "lighten the labor itself" (*op. mon.* 17.20). We have to think of our labor making possible our spiritual pursuits while still acknowledging that the two are not synonymous. For example, labor properly organized and carried out provides workers with an opportunity to love their neighbor as themselves, thereby loving God in and through their neighbor relations. Augustine is thus suggesting that in directing their labor toward these inner (spiritual) ends, the labor can be undertaken in order to enable and further their knowledge and love of God.

The potential of this alternative vision of labor is, indeed, most readily visible in the context of the monastery. When situated in the broader context of the monastery, the basic dynamics animating labor are liturgically structured. Labor is positioned within the larger liturgy of the day, which provides monks with sharp enough boundaries to protect against overwork or any overestimation of one's labor. Monastic labor is also framed in communal terms; the needs and well-being of the community at large depend on, in a very real way, the labor of each individual comprising that community. It makes sense, then, that Augustine's practical advice to the striking monks is to abandon the strict divide they have erected between prayer and labor. They should, rather, take up labor on behalf of their community in prayerful terms. Within such a vision, each aspect of the monks' life—prayer, study, labor, and communal belonging—plays a constitutive role in spiritual formation.

In order to elucidate the full potential of Augustine's treatment of monastic labor—something more akin to a mode of life rather than a singular, limited action—we must briefly explore Pierre Hadot's famous distinction between philosophical discourse and a philosophical life in *What is Ancient Philosophy*. Philosophical discourse was a crucial, extraordinary set of reflections on theories of knowledge, logic, and physics, but Hadot urged his readers to understand (ancient) philosophy as something altogether different. Hadot attempted to have his readers situate those theoretical systems within the larger context of a form of life. That form of life was not, he writes, "located at the end of the process of philosophical activity, like a kind of accessory or appendix. On the contrary, it stands at the beginning, in a complex interrelationship with critical reaction to other existential attitudes" (Hadot 2002, 3 n. 3). Philosophy, then, necessarily entails a series of existential commitments that structure one's life in the world, and philosophical discourse is but a singular (though crucial) component of that form of life. Anyone who attempted to undertake the theoretical discourse apart from the form of life was traditionally understood to be a Sophist (Hadot 2002, 174).

A similar kind of contextualization is necessary to grasp the potential of Augustine's treatment of monastic labor. This is a form of labor whose meaning is only fully legible when taken in conjunction with the larger life of liturgy that the monastery sought to foster. The emphasis should be on the form of life the liturgy makes possible rather than the liturgy itself. When labor is undertaken in this manner, it is possible for the boundaries between labor and prayer to blur, such that the whole of one's labor is grafted into their larger life of prayer before God. Under such conditions, labor can become a modality of prayer. This is labor for the sake of prayer, undertaken in hope of the time in which *sapientia* will displace productive activity altogether in the eschaton (Luke 10; *Trin* 1.20; S. 104, 81–7).

The goodness of this transformed labor does not stem from its location within the monastic walls; rather, that labor is good to the extent that it is directed towards the proper end and animated by the theological virtues. This is why, for Augustine, something of the monastic approach to labor is readily available to those outside the monastic context. This is particularly true given that the theological virtues of faith, hope, and love are intrinsic to the life of the believer and provide something of a structure and framework of Christian existence (Mathewes 2008, 20). It is thus to grace's transformation of labor (in and through the virtues) that we must now turn.

The Virtues and Transformation

As Oliver O'Donovan has recently shown, the theological virtues, being animated as they are by grace and made available to all believers regardless of their location in time-space, have much to teach us about the ways in which we undertake our labor today (O. O'Donovan 2017, 102–34). Rooting that difference in virtue—or, more precisely, in the difference virtues make in the life of believers—is significant in that virtue is not spatially or temporally bound, which demonstrates the potential of such transformations and possibilities outside of the monastic context.

Additionally, the difference(s) made in virtue does not stem from human agency alone. That is, the virtues are not positive accomplishments of self-making. Augustine is, after all, quite critical of Pelagian understandings of humanity's moral potential (Mathewes 2008, 16 n. 61). The alternative mode of labor Augustine is sketching here is a mode of agency undertaken in response to God and God's efficacious gift of transformative grace (Mathewes 2003, 9).

But, as we established previously, one is incapable of acting virtuously in and of their own volition while in a sinful state. This is why Augustine insists that there cannot be any cultivation of virtue apart from grace, which communicates the knowledge and love of God to the sinful soul in a transformative manner. And this is why Augustine's criticism of Cicero's virtuous statesman in *De civitate dei* (*civ. Dei.*) is such a crucial piece of Augustine's larger criticism of Rome's misdirected (and inherently limited) civic virtues. In a classic, Aristotelian manner, that statesman would be considered fit for leadership to the extent that he embodied the highest virtues and ideals of the community he was leading. In so doing, Cicero's ideal statesman exemplifies justice and thereby encourages the broader community to pursue justice as well. Augustine, on the other hand, argues that the capacity for true virtue and justice depends on the healing of a leader's soul, such that their fundamental limitations resulting from sin are overcome (*civ. Dei.* 19.23–7; Dodaro 2008, 31 n. 23). Hence, Augustine's insistence that Christ himself is the true philosophy capable of fostering virtue during our lives in the world (*civ. Dei.* 17.4, 9.17, and 10.24; Dodaro 2008, 31, 73).

Augustine insists throughout *civ. Dei.* that any acquisition of true virtue is only ever made possible by God's giving of grace, which pardons the sinner and transforms the soul's capacities. The virtues of faith and humility, enabled as they are by grace, help counteract the ignorance and weakness that result from sin. Faith directs the soul toward both the enjoyment of God and a proper use of the world, and humility overcomes the self's reliance of its own strength when pursuing such ultimate ends. True virtue is thus always aimed at eternal goods, and it therefore takes aim at the knowledge and love of God, who is the highest good and source of goodness itself. This is why Augustine argues that any justice a statesman can carry out will be accompanied by a public testimony regarding their own corruption and vices (Dodaro 2008, 35 n. 23). It is only in grace that one's virtues are transformed and redirected toward real justice and goodness. And it is precisely because the virtues stem from grace that one's own motivations and actions are only explicable in reference to the love of God (Mathewes 2008, 135 n. 59).

In that vein, I do not mean to imply or suggest that non-Christians are necessarily bound to a life of labor marked by injustice and misery, and I believe Augustine's treatment of the possibilities and limits of non-Christians' virtues renders such a claim incoherent. There is no doubt that someone with no confessed interest in Christ can alter the temporal, relational, and formative dynamics of their labor and professional life in ways that largely correspond to the effects outlined above and below. They can and should do so. My point, rather, is that the grace making possible a virtuous life for the Christian can and should lead to such changes. The end result of that gracious transformation is that the Christian's labor (again, when properly, virtuously undertaken) can become a mode of prayer and a site of grace's transformation in the life of the believer. This is a key distinction for the Augustinian, though I suspect the non-Christian would have little interest in the ends with which Augustine is so concerned. Consider the way Augustine infamously picks up on Cicero's distinction between a virtue's *telos* and its appropriate actions (*civ. Dei.* 10.18). As we see in his analysis of Rome's glorious heroes, certain seemingly good actions can emerge from selfish motivations, which is to say that the same action can be undertaken in distinct ways depending on the ends toward which it is undertaken (*civ. Dei.* 5.19). To whatever extent the appropriate action emerges from a desire for self-love rather than the love of God (and love of neighbor a true love of God motivates), those actions are properly characterized as a kind of vice. Hence the category we now refer to as "pagan virtues," or "splendid vices" (Dodaro 2008, 27–71; 2004; Rist 1997, 168–73; Harding 2008; Gaul 2009). It must be stressed, though, that to whatever extent a non-Christian is interested in taking on these kinds of temporal, relational, and formational dynamics in their labor, they will be largely indistinguishable from the virtuous Christian, who is experiencing transformation of those same dynamics by way of God's gift of grace (Tornau 2019, 7.2). Perhaps this is one reason (of many) that Augustine acknowledges the church remains indistinguishable from the earthly city during the *saeculum*.

The virtues are, ultimately, a matter of preparation. In our lives in the world, we are being prepared for and made worthy of what is to come in the new creation. In so doing, they work on our dispositions and teach us to be more open to God's grace (Mathewes 2008, 12–13). That is, we are being made fit for a life in which we take a full share in God's beauty and goodness, and we come to inhabit such modes of being in and through the virtues, taking a share through the transformation that makes possible a proper use of the world. It is in that transformation that a deep sense of desire for the life to come is cultivated, particularly given that the world cannot fully provide such joy (Mathewes 2008, 167).

This matters for the question of labor in that this virtuous transformation makes possible alternative ways of being and doing in the world, such that the same activities are properly undertaken and redirected toward the love of God and others. As I will show in the following section, that distinction has much to offer Christians navigating a world largely structured by finance-dominated capitalism, particularly when considering a Christian treatment of labor.

Liturgical Labor

We become instruments of God in the world when we love God properly, and this proper love of God manifests in terms of a proper love of one's self and others. When our love is transformed in this way, we "use" things, people, and ourselves properly by loving them in God. On this point, Charles Mathewes writes, "As regards people, one discovers that caritas is community-building: as this energy directs the self toward conversion back to God, it also urges the self to seek communion with others" (Mathewes 2008, 81). After all, Augustine's instruction to "love and do what you will" accounts for the transformation of one's affections (*Ep. Jo.* 7.8). He means to say that "love has so transformed you that you now behave in a new way" (Mathewes 2008, 82). The task of this section is to plainly demonstrate the difference that transformation should make in our experience of time, relationality, and selfhood.

Grace transforms the believer to the extent that they can undertake labor in a virtuous manner, and labor is hereby reoriented toward enjoyment of God, proper use of the world, and love of others. This transformation is most easily identifiable in the context of the monastery, particularly in the modes of time, relationality, and selfhood fostered therein. But, as was argued above, the grace and virtues that enable this transformation of labor are not confined to the walls of the monastery, and that same grace and virtue can and should inform a transformed labor in our contemporary world, even outside of monastery walls. Much of his theological treatment of labor suggests that this alternative approach to labor is distinctly possible outside the walls of the monastery.

"Liturgical labor" is a mode of labor made possible by the transformative power of grace. It is the labor of the transformed self, wherein one's disordered loves are redirected to the extent that one properly uses others, the world, and one's self for the enjoyment of God. When grace transforms our loves and desires, labor takes on a new meaning and shape. Such grace-enabled labor, undertaken as it will be in virtue, has the ability to further enable that love, preparing the self for further transformation into the life of God. This potential can be manifested in our relationship to time, others, and the self.

First, liturgical labor ticks to a different time and should enable us to rethink our labor time in constructive ways. Varied workplaces (i.e. shop floors, corner offices, classrooms, secretarial desks, delivery cars, coffee shops, and cubicles) each have their own secular liturgies wherein time is ordered and thereby ritualized (Lofton 2017, 34–59). Much like the way one labors for a fixed period of time and is expected to drop one's labor and return to prayer at regularly scheduled intervals in the context of the monastery, liturgical labor has the potential to redirect these secular liturgies toward different ends. In so doing, liturgical labor transforms our conceptions of time by delimiting our drives toward productivity and placing the hour of labor within the larger liturgical movement of the day. Outcomes, deadlines, and productive thresholds become much less important than the ends to which they are directed.

Second, liturgical labor, being communally oriented, fosters new forms of relationality. In the monastic context, labor is divided according to the needs of the community at large. In the context of the monastery, we know that old social and class divisions gave way to a new social arrangement wherein the value and dignity of each was valued apart from their productive output (P. Brown 2012, 176–7). This is particularly significant given the rigid nature of social classes in late antiquity (Arbesmann 1973, 259). Given that the monks own everything in common, each one's labor is freed to be carried out in service of the community's good and needs. Within such a context, self-interest is expanded to communal self-interest as laborers come to see their place and needs within the larger whole of the community in which they are participating. Where competition might have previously reigned supreme, such modes of labor overcome those communal limitations by prioritizing the well-being of the community at large (Berry 2010; 2019a,b). To the extent that we cultivate similar desires and ends in our working relationships, we too can see new forms of relationality emerge.

And thirdly, liturgical labor fosters a unique form of formation and selfhood. As has been previously established, Augustine argues that we are constituted in and through our loves. We are ultimately oriented toward God even if our disordered desires lead us to pursue other ends. But in and through grace, those misdirected, disordered desires and loves are reoriented such that we properly use the world in and for our enjoyment of God. Liturgical labor is thus a byproduct of this reorientation. Augustine also reminds us that the Lord is providing for us in and through our labor (*Op. mon.* 26.35). It is a gift that we are the type of thing capable of laboring, and Augustine reminds the striking monks that God might be seeking to provide for those in need through the labor of the monks. Even more particularly, Augustine insists that God is the very ground of our own agential capacities. As Augustine notes, *"[n]either the one who plants is anything nor the one who waters, but the one who gives the growth, God* (1 Cor. 3:7), because the labor and skill applied from the outside are applied by one who also was nonetheless created and is being governed and directed invisibly by God" (*Gn. litt.* 8.8.16). That is, while humans certainly labor in order to feed and clothe themselves, it is through God as the ground of being that they move at all. Such a vision features a sort of confluence of agencies, as God's agency and will are carried out in and through our own (*Op. mon.* 27).

A similar kind of contextualization is necessary to grasp the potential of Augustine's treatment of monastic labor. This is a form of labor whose meaning is only fully legible when taken in conjunction with the larger life of liturgy that the monastery sought to foster. The emphasis should be on the form of life the liturgy makes possible rather than the liturgy itself. When labor is undertaken in this manner, it is possible for the boundaries between labor and prayer to blur, such that the whole of one's labor is grafted into their larger life of prayer before God. Under such conditions, labor can become a modality of prayer. This is labor for the sake of prayer, undertaken in hope of the time in which *sapientia* will displace productive activity altogether in the eschaton (Luke 10; *Trin.* I.).

Conclusion: Properly Related to, Directed, Undertaken, and Contextualized

The most basic task of this chapter has been to identify some insights in Augustine's nonsystematic treatment of labor that I believe can and should inform a properly theological treatment of labor. Augustine, I have argued, offers us the resources to theorize the spiritual and moral possibilities of labor when it is properly contextualized, understood, related to, and undertaken. This is precisely why the monastery supplies such a unique context through which to imagine this potential. Put differently, Augustine's theological system provides us with some resources through which we might distinguish between the goods of a particular labor opportunity and its moral limitations, but he also offers us readers some clear guidelines through which the former might be undertaken and the latter overcome.

"Liturgical labor," I have argued, is a mode of labor made possible by the transformative power of grace that can and should contest the operative norms and power dynamics animating labor in contemporary capitalism. It is the labor of the transformed self, wherein one's disordered loves are redirected to the extent that one properly uses others, the world, and one's self for the enjoyment of God. When grace transforms our loves and desires, labor takes on a new meaning and shape, and that new shape (i.e., labor being situated in a broader life of liturgy) features a new relation to time, others, ourselves, and God.

When undertaken in those circumstances, work can and should play a crucial role in one's temporal progression toward the beatific vision, even if that progression depends on properly relating to, directing, undertaking, and contextualizing the work. That is, the content and manner in which the work is done makes the difference. And to think about that possibility with Augustine is to insist that that difference is only ever made possible but the transformative power of grace.

Such labor would be, similar to Pierre Hadot's famous distinction between philosophical discourse and a philosophical life, but one element of a holistic life dedicated to the love and service of God. The context of and relation to that labor situates it within a larger life of Christian formation, such that labor can become a modality of prayer.

This matters, in that Augustine gives us the resources to theorize the spiritual and moral possibilities of labor when it is properly related to, directed, undertaken, and contextualized. This is a form of labor based on a proper love of oneself before God, the world, and others, and proper love of the creature (oneself or another) in service of one's love of God leads to a shift from lust to charity (*Trin.* 9.13). Laboring in charity depends on properly relating to, directing, undertaking, and contextualizing that labor; the significance of those qualifiers cannot be overstated. I am by no means suggesting that standard labor practices can become modes of prayer if one simply works hard enough, as though the problems of our contemporary labor structures can be put aside in and through self-discipline or crude self-care practices. Rather, the ways in which the labor is related to, directed, undertaken, and contextualized make all the difference. This is, rather, a kind of labor distinct from the standard norms of contemporary capitalism, and playing out the transformed dynamics of this kind of labor (time, relationality, self) would necessarily entail a kind of deformation from the operative norms and ends of our economy's status quo. And so it makes a kind of Augustinian sense to claim, as I am, that the extent to which there is any potential for spiritual and moral reformation in labor largely depends on properly navigating labor relations (to labor itself, to those labored with, to ourselves in labor, to the objects of our labor).

5

The Abolition of Work

But the Lord answered her, "Martha, Martha, you are worried and distracted by many things; there is need of only one thing. Mary has chosen the better part, which will not be taken away from her."

LK. 10:42

Rest and quiet is worth more than any activity

AUGUSTINE
DE GENESI AD LITTERAM

Introduction

In this, the fifth and final chapter, I develop a constructive, Augustinian treatment of the end of work. I draw on Augustine's reading of Mary and Martha's competing agencies in Luke 10 to characterize work as a distinctly human, sinful phenomenon that must be endured during our lives in the world, even as we hope for its eventual abolition in the eschaton. Such an approach clarifies some of the problems with our current understanding of and relation to work while also implicitly prescribing some constructive alternatives. The basic task of this chapter is to articulate the critical and constructive work-related implications of Augustine's interpretation of Luke 10.

In order to accomplish that goal, I begin in the first section with a brief overview of Augustine's interpretation of Luke 10. He reads Mary and Martha as being representative of competing modes of agency. Martha represents the mundane, fleeting, necessary tasks that are part and parcel of our lives in the world. And Mary represents the tranquility and unproductive rest that will characterize when we eventually see God face to face; we might call this the beatific vision, heaven, or the eschaton. As such, Augustine's read of the Lukan account of Mary and Martha has fascinating and helpful implications for our understanding of work. In such a reading work is a distinctly human, sinful phenomenon (at least as we experience it today) that simply has to be endured for now. It will eventually be abolished altogether, as the restful contemplation of God is clearly to be prioritized, and we are to work in hope of that eventual end.

That Lukan account puts a pressing question to us: How do we undertake the necessary tasks of Martha in full awareness that (1) Mary chose the better, (2) Mary's presence with Christ rightfully displaced her responsibility for life's mundane tasks, and (3) Martha's work will eventually be put aside altogether? Put differently, how ought we carry out Martha's work in hope of being like Mary? And what does Jesus' prioritization of Mary's agency and choice reveal about our own work-related assumptions?

The task of the second section is to begin answering that cluster of questions. Mary's rest, when read today, serves to contest our commitment to overwork. The Lukan passage reminds us that hard work is the result of the fall and therefore an effect of the fallen order from which God is redeeming humanity (*civ. Dei.* XXII.22; Arbesmann 1973, 250). In fact, Mary represents a kind of unproductive rest that is good through and through: she simply rests and enjoys God. In that same vein, the Lukan passage contests our obsession with productive output and urges us to move beyond our limited, productivity-driven work ethics. This approach relativizes economic value and contests our overestimation of productive agency in the economic sphere.

But Martha's work and Mary's rest do more than reveal the limitations of our own cultural assumptions regarding work. The passage also spells out some practicalities for navigating contemporary economic life in ways that avoid both escapism and any overestimation of economic agency or justice. In the third section, I will articulate the implications of undertaking work in terms of worship.

First, Christ's rebuke of Martha clarifies for us the import of being prepared for faithful work in and through liturgical formation. That is, working faithfully requires situating our work within a larger life of moral formation and communal membership. Being formed in and through the life of the church should help—though not ultimately resolve—our tendency toward unhealthy work.

Second, Mary and Martha represent twin poles of worship and work and thereby counsel us to decouple our understanding of vocation from professional work-life. The Christian's vocation will always transcend their professional endeavors. The gap between these two poles might be smaller in some ideal settings than others, but a gap will always remain. And Christians concerned with teasing out the economic implications of worship of God must shift our talk of vocation accordingly.

Third, and perhaps most simply, Mary and Martha call us to increased sabbath. This is not a thicker idea of sabbath, as much as it is more sabbath time. That is, the Lukan passage makes clear we simply need to work less so as to prioritize "choosing the better."

Fourth, faithful work must be undertaken for the common good. The potential mundanities and drudgery of Martha's tasks are given new life and meaning when they are undertaken for the good of others, for the life of the whole, particularly when read in relation to Augustine's understanding of the close relationship between love of God and neighbor.

At this point in the chapter, a few caveats will be in order. Mine is not an individualistic proposal, as though praying and going to church can make one's work life and work relations faithful. As I have previously named there are structural and cultural realities that foster unhealthy modes of attachment and relationship in our work. Thinking extensively about Augustine's vision of work and his understanding of attachment requires we rethink some of those basic structures so as to create more potential for working faithfully. Additionally, avoiding any structural analysis runs the risk of justifying the sinful, unjust practices of our present economic order. This is not a Christian vision for some nonexisting utopia that ultimately collapses into a legitimation of the present order.

In order to demonstrate some of the structural issues that must be altered and the viability of such shifts in the here and now (yes, even amid millennial capitalism and a neoliberal order), I will conclude the chapter with a brief examination of one particular type of cooperative business structure: the worker self-directed enterprise. Doing so, I believe clarifies one viable means through which the most practical implications of the Lukan passage can be carried out.

Reading Luke 10

In the first book of *De Trinitate*, Augustine uses the story of Mary and Martha in Luke 10 to compare and contrast two competing visions of human agency in relation to humanity's final calling:

> Now as they went on their way, he entered a certain village, where a woman named Martha welcomed him into her home. She had a sister named Mary, who sat at the Lord's feet and listened to what he was saying. But Martha was distracted by her many tasks; so she came to him and asked, "Lord, do you not care that my sister has left me to do all the work by myself? Tell her then to help me." But the Lord answered her, "Martha, Martha, you are worried and distracted by many things; there is need of only one thing. Mary has chosen the better part, which will not be taken away from her." (Lk. 10:38-42)

According to Luke, when Jesus visits the home of Martha, Martha spends her precious time in the presence of Jesus playing the role of host. Her sister Mary, however, spent that time sitting at Jesus' feet, apparently captivated by what he was saying. Martha—who felt (understandably) abandoned to tend to the tasks that make possible hosting a prophet and the crowd that follows such prophets around all by herself—approaches Jesus and asks if he cares that she has been abandoned "to do all the work by [herself]." If he does, she says, then he should tell Mary to get up and help. In response to what feels like a very human and understandable set of frustrations, Jesus tells Martha that she is unduly distracted by her need to carry out her various tasks. There is actually "only one thing," Jesus explains, and "Mary has chosen the better part, which will not be taken away from her."[1]

---

[1] It is also worth noting that this is the same Mary—the sister of Martha and Lazarus—that will eventually wash Jesus' feet with her tears and hair (see Mt. 26:6-13, Mk 14:3-9, Lk. 7:36-50, and Jn 12:1-8). In that narrative, Judas protests her

The Luke passage comes up in Augustine's *De Trinitate* as an example of the sort of contemplation and presence that constitutes the beatific vision—"the direct contemplation of God, in which all good actions have their end, and there is everlasting rest and joy that shall not be taken away from us"(*Trin.* I.10.20). In Augustine's telling, Mary symbolizes that joy and contemplation which the faithful will eventually undertake in an unceasing manner. It is Mary, at the Lord's feet, intent upon the Lord's words and "at rest from all activity and intent upon the truth" that images our final, eternal calling. In Augustine's telling, while "Martha was preparing a banquet for the Lord, Mary was already reveling in the banquet of the Lord" (*S.* 104). It is Mary's contemplative agency that most clearly resembles our eschatological end; burdened work, after all, is nothing except the result of a sinful world (*Trin.* I.10.20). As such, it will be abolished upon Christ's return.

It is important to note, though, that Augustine does not vilify or condemn Martha's work. Martha was "busy doing what had to be done—activity which though good and useful is going to end one day and give place to rest" (*Trin.* I.3.10.20) The point for Augustine is not that Martha chose the bad option; it is that Mary chose the better (*S.* 103). If anything, Augustine legitimates Martha in a way that Jesus does not, at least in the passage given to us in Luke. Martha is simply doing what needs doing, and the language Augustine uses to characterize Martha's toil—with connotations of both work and suffering—is sympathetic (Ernst 2009, 217). He thereby positions Martha as a symbol for the active life during our lives in the world while we await Christ's return. The curse of toilsome work has not yet been abolished, Augustine suggests, and Martha is not to be faulted for acknowledging the necessity of such work-related duties (*Trin.* I.3.10.20). Crucial for Augustine's analysis is the insight that Martha's mode of agency will ultimately end; Jesus explicitly notes as much. The toil of work will pass away, the unity of charity will remain. The task that remains for us until

---

economic misstep much like Martha did. Surely, Judas insists, she has misvalued both her own agency and this costly perfume. But once again, Jesus affirms Mary's economic logic, which defied cultural and economic norms. Her sense of value is shaped by the presence of Christ, which places her outside the norm with regard to her estimation of costly goods, her own agency, rest, and gifts.

that ultimate abolition is to figure out how to navigate the toilsome demands of bodily life (*S.* 104).

The Lukan account of Mary and Martha—and Augustine's interpretation of the text—has fascinating implications for my own analysis of work. Mary is a representative of humanity's highest, contemplative pursuits, whereas Martha represents the unfortunate economic realities of a life carried out in a sinful world. Augustine thus prioritizes Mary's contemplative, worshipful refusal of work while simultaneously noting the realities of inhabiting a sinful world wherein work is cursed and still necessary. These competing visions can be read as a theological treatment of work as a distinctly human phenomenon.

Mary's vision is not altogether unavailable to us today, even as we continue waiting on Christ's return. Augustine even says as much when referencing Mary's rest in Sermon 104: "Even now, you see, we do enjoy something of that sort" (*S. 104*). To substantiate that claim he points out that each member of the congregation that is present, gathered together in time and space to hear whatever witness the saint offers, has left their shops and offices. They have put down the things of work to gather for worship, thereby moving from the figure of Martha to that of Mary (*S.* 104).

Within a sinful world, work takes on the same role of moral reformation that Augustine recognizes in any other form of worldly suffering (*civ. Dei.* XVIII.49). Work, he maintains, is considered honorable whenever it provides humanity with the required necessities for sustaining life, is done well, and is carried out honestly (a rather tall order given the toilsome, cursed nature of work in the wake of the fall) (Arbesmann 1973, 252). This is why he argues that the work of artisans is preferable to that of merchants or managers. Doing manual work—occupying one's mind with the task at hand and thereby avoiding thoughts of profit and accumulation—is said to be a higher good than delegating such tasks (certainly management is its own form of work, Augustine notes), thereby risking the occupation of one's mind with anxiety, possession, or excess money (*op. mon.* 15.16).

For Augustine, happiness is attained eschatologically; it is emphatically not readily available during our lives in the world. The city of God, he explains, will enter into the fullness of joy only when it encounters Christ face to face in the wake of his return.

The city of God's pilgrimage in the world, then, is marked by hope of that coming future, and it must therefore journey with patient anticipation of what will be but is not yet. Citizens of that city are patiently to endure the evils that characterize a fallen world "until we attain those goods where everything will afford us inexpressible delight and there will be nothing left that we have to endure" (*civ. Dei*. XIV.4). Maintaining hope thus depends on properly navigating the finitude of the world and its evils. While Augustine thinks that the evils of any age are ultimately traced back to the consequences of sin, life itself is now "constricted by the bonds of death." The earthly city inevitably organizes society according to pride and domination rather than justice under God's rule.

Rather than seeking to construct or identify some lasting mode of happiness in that context, Augustine argues that Christians should name their misery and cry out to God for help: "How much more perceptive it would be, how much more worthy of a human being, for him to recognize the human misery laid bare by those necessities, to detest that misery's grip on him, and, if he is devout in his wisdom, to cry out to God, Deliver me from my necessities (PS 15:17)!" (*civ. Dei*. XIX.4). Christians must patiently and wisely endure "the woes which this condemned life has deserved, having the foresight to be thankful that it will all come to an end, faithfully and patiently awaiting the happiness which the emancipated life of the future is going to have without end" (*Trin*. XII.16.20). The task of being Christian must be characterized by a certain endurance of suffering, a learning to suffer the inevitable distension that results from being in such a time and being in time itself (*conf*. 11; Mathewes 2008, 10–12, 32).

Additionally, the faithful are to train in virtue in order properly to endure the pains of the world and be prepared for the new age to come. Growth in virtue, which Augustine repeatedly argues is only ever made possible by the grace of Christ, can and does lead to earthly peace, to the extent that it is possible for humans to have such peace. As Augustine notes, "Virtue is true virtue only when it directs all the goods of which it makes good use, and directs all that it does in making good use of both goods and evils, and directs itself as well, to the end where our peace will be so unsurpassed that it could not possibly be better or greater" (*civ*. XIX.10). That earthly peace—to the extent it is possible—depends on a properly ordered set of loves that gives rise to an appropriate relation to the city's temporal goods (i.e., their production, distribution, use, and understanding).

Faithful Christian political and economic life, in this model, entails attempting to "stand out from" the norms of operative society without overestimating the potential of inaugurating some alternative, Christian utopia (P. Brown 2013, 338–9). Earthly peace thus depends on accepting the limited range of possibilities for happiness in this life while at the same time seeking to navigate the finitude of the world in light of the justice and love that characterizes the coming age. As such, our hope of resting with Mary—a mode of unceasing rest into which, Augustine insists, all saints will eventually move—can and should inform our work in the present. Our work no longer resembles joyful gardening, and yet work has not yet been altogether abolished. For Augustine, we must undergo the suffering of our contemporary work-life in hope of its eventual abolition.

The point here is that we should navigate the demands of economic life in the world in hope of the abolition of those demands (S. 104). Such demands, he crucially notes, are to be tolerated rather than loved (S. 104). The question of work thus becomes how we should inhabit Mary's rest in the midst of a system that demands Martha's work. And, when necessary, how do we undertake Martha's tasks in ways that circumvent the system that prioritized the disciples' rest at the expense of Martha's time and energy? Or, to translate those questions into a contemporary idiom, how do we inhabit Mary's rest in a culture that solely prioritizes Martha's productivity? What might it mean to undertake Martha's activities in and for the sake of the enjoyment Mary has already taken a share in?

Challenging Our Work Culture

While Augustine's read of Luke 10—and the passage itself— are fascinating in their own right, they also contain a number of pressing implications regarding our cultural understanding of work. Those implications are prescient for the project at hand given my previous articulation of a problematic cultural understanding of work. As I explained in the introduction, we have built a culture wherein our life's meaning is functionally inseparable from our professional endeavors, successes, and failures. Who would I be if not in my present role? And how might my sense of self be revolutionized if I really did step into that new role? Overwork is ubiquitous, and it is made possible by constant drives for efficiency, productivity, new projects, and expansion. In our time of rest, we question the ways our economic norms and structures further create inequality and oppression, and yet we continue working at alarming rates nonetheless. Rarely do we ever question precisely why we are so obsessed with our work.

Against this painfully obvious set of cultural norms, Augustine's reading of Mary and Martha's two modes of agency offers us an alternative vision from which we reconsider our relationship to work and the cultural assumptions that sustain that relationship. In this section, I will critically deploy those Augustinian insights in order to contest our work culture. I will name what I take to be the three most pressing ways that Augustine's vision of Jesus' response to Mary and Martha should change how we think about our work and productive lives: contesting overwork, rethinking value, and breaking our deeply ingrained work ethic.

Contesting Overwork

The first piece of our work culture that Augustine's reading of Luke 10 challenges is our constant overwork. With the advent of digital technologies and the ubiquity of email, the boundaries between work-time and not-work-time are more ambiguous and permeable than ever before. American workers spend more time working than ever before, and an increasing demand that nonworking time be productive for work has created a culture of burnout, exhaustion, and instability. Augustine's reading of Luke 10 offers a compelling alternative.

In Augustine's telling, we are actually created for purposelessness. Or, maybe more accurately, for nothing productive. Joy and delight rest at the heart of the grace that comes to us as good news. We are created to delight in God, for God's own delight, and nothing we can do in and through our own capacities is capable of enabling such enjoyment (Mathewes

2004, 214; Williams 2016b). That is, we are ultimately created to delight in a God who has no need for us, and nothing we can do is to be considered more valuable or important than such endless delight (Mathewes 2004, 213–14). We are certainly called to reform ourselves into the image of God through our own active, deliberate agencies, but we mistake our own natures and capacities when we assume we can produce or actualize something of ourselves in and through our own agencies, ideas, or practices (Tanner 2019, 207). In fact, Christians traditionally recognize that toilsome work and hard work is the result of the fall; work is a form of punishment and therefore part of the cluster of realities from which God is redeeming humanity (*civ. Dei.* XXII.22; Arbesmann 1973, 250). As we see in Augustine's Genesis commentaries, Adam and Eve did something comparable to working in the garden, but it was totally free of toil. He writes, "Labor was not a hardship then, but a spontaneous experience of joy. The things created by God grew more exuberantly and fruitfully through the concurrent labor of man, resulting in more copious praise of the Creator himself" (*Gn. litt.* 249). It is only after the fall that work becomes a hard, toilsome activity marked by a divine curse. To think with Augustine about Mary and Martha in relation to work is to insist that our work must be used in service of our enjoyment of God; the former shall end and the latter will last.

Augustine writes, "No one ought to be so completely at leisure that in his leisure he takes no thought for serving his neighbor, nor should anyone be so fully active that he makes no room for the contemplation of God" (*civ. Dei.* XIV.19). It is not, in fact, the activities of work or leisure themselves that are to be properly enjoyed; those modes of agency, important as they might be for our life during the world, are only to be used in God so as to make possible our enjoyment of God (*civ. Dei.* XIV.19). We are created to delight in God, for God's delight first and foremost, which is simultaneously our own derivative delight as well (Mathewes 2004, 214; Williams 2016c). Worship thus brackets work by insisting that work has no meaning apart from its reference to God; work must come to an end in order to make space and time for more formative pursuits. That cluster of insights is a direct challenge to contemporary productivism and the contemporary work ethics this project aims to problematize.

Rethinking Value

The second piece of our work culture that Augustine's reading of Luke 10 challenges is a sense of value. This Augustinian approach to work insists that our productive work is not itself the primary source of value in the world. As Kathryn Tanner has recently noted, "The materials upon which we work have value prior to our activity insofar as they form the non-purposive 'products' of God's creative activity" (Tanner 2019, 208). Given the nature of God's creation and preservation, Augustine notes that it is for good reason that we do not treat farmers as the sole creators of their crops. As previously established, the series of acts by which farmers grow crops—while certainly toilsome, demanding, and fragile—is fostering the actualization of a potentiality that exists exterior the farmer herself. For Augustine, God is the ground of the potential and process through which a seed becomes a bush yielding fruit, even if that occurs through and depends upon the correlating agency of the farmer (Hill 2004, 5.6.18; 285). In this sense, the worker (who depends on God for their being, agency, and own range of potentialities) only ever formalizes or organizes preexisting material, which also derives its existence from God. God can thus be said to have created the craftsperson's body, the mind that animates and exerts some form of control over that body, the very materials the mind directs the body to work upon, and the skill and capacity that enables a creative worker to visualize and actualize a plan (*conf.* XI.5.7). The goodness of any action or thing thus ultimately stems from God's own goodness. Such an approach recognizes the potential and creative goodness of humans transforming objects of nature through their own productive capacities for the sake of addressing a pressing need. But this Augustinian ethic insists that any productive act humanity undertakes always already depends on a distinctly transcendent God for its viability and possibility (Tanner 2004, 46). Value simply does not enter the world exclusively through my own agential capacities, as though my own work were some portal to divinity; use-value always depends on a generous, transcendent God that created the stuff being worked on as well as the potentiality of human agency that transforms that preexisting natural entity (Tanner 2019, 208).

Overcoming Our Work Ethic

The third element of our work culture that Augustine's reading of Luke 10 challenges is our obsession with productive output.

Recall Derek Thompson's diagnosis of "workism" that I briefly pointed to in the introduction. Thompson points to a sizeable pool of data that demonstrates that Americans work more, take fewer vacations, retire later, and we do so while receiving less unemployment, disability, and retirement benefits than comparably rich nations. We average more hours worked in a year than any other comparably developed country. We tend to believe that work is crucial for all aspects of economic production, that it is the centerpiece of our identities, and that the best way to promote personal and communal welfare is more work. These are deeply held cultural commitments (Thompson 2019, 1.2).

And such assumptions have transitioned beyond mere norms and preferences into moral commitments. It's not so much that we simply prefer to work more; we believe we ought to log more hours, and we think everyone else should too. Hence the phrase "work ethic." We celebrate the innovators and trailblazers who build things through non-stop work, and we do so without questioning the costs or effects on their nonworking lives. Conversely, we judge and condemn those that we believe are not working enough. We associate one's "deservedness" with productive output, and we thereby denigrate those that are not as committed to their working lives. Philosopher Kathi Weeks has described this work ethic as "productivist," referring to our deeply held belief that one ought to be producing and working more and more. We prioritize getting things done, we celebrate efficiency and results, and we have convinced ourselves that productive activity in the workplace is to be prioritized above all else. Rest is simply for the sake of recouping, and our "productivist" tendencies push us to cut into that rest for the sake of extra productivity. Within a productivist culture, time is rendered as the opportunity to undertake that next task (Weeks 2011, 12).

But as Kathryn Tanner has persuasively noted, this does not make theological sense. God's creation and salvation of humans are emphatically not for the sake of them undertaking some additional productive activity (Tanner 2019, 206). God's agency is itself nonproductive in this sense: "The fundamentally non-purposive, and in that sense non-productive, activity of God should underlie all our productive activity, assuring its fundamental value, whatever our particular capacities and their measure of success" (Tanner 2019, 208).

Against these norms, the Augustinian vision of Mary and Martha insists that productive output should have no bearing on my relation with others. To value my neighbor in terms of their productive potential is, for Augustine, to fail to love them humanely. And to consider myself in terms of my productive output (i.e., "What did I get done today?") is to misconstrue our vocation entirely. Part of the Christian economic task is to cultivate earthly peace to whatever extent possible in order that my neighbor's livelihood, survival, and earthly peace are not conditional upon any form of productive output.

The Limits of Vocation

The implications of Augustine's read of Luke 10 are not merely negative. That is, Martha's work and Mary's rest do something more than reveal the limitations of our own cultural assumptions regarding work. The passage also spells out some practicalities for navigating contemporary economic life that avoids both escapism and any overestimation of economic agency or justice. In this third section, I spell out a few of those most pressing practicalities. I do so by naming what I take to be the limits of "vocation," the primary path these conversations tend to travel. In contrast, I articulate a constructive treatment of the work-related implications of worship, which both challenge our typical understandings of the term and helpfully frame the positive vision of work I am calling for here.

Most particularly, I want to make the case that an Augustinian vision of vocation and the dynamics impacting ethical work require we think beyond the present norms structuring our economic lives. We are to undertake the work of Martha in a way that's directed and shaped by the worshipful rest of Mary, to the extent possible. Such an endeavor, I think, requires we think about common treatments of vocation and the context in which work is typically carried out.

What We Mean When We Say "Vocation"

Much of our popular conception of "vocation" is downstream from
the Protestant Reformation. In a time when a sense of "calling" was
typically in reference to holy orders, the monastery, or some specific
religious activity, Martin Luther celebrated the holy mundanity of
everyday work. The activity was good when "a man works at his
trade, walks, stands, eats, drinks, sleeps, and does all kinds of works
for the nourishment of his body or for the common welfare" (Luther
2012, III). For Luther, faith obliterated any kind of hierarchy that
positioned religious work as more holy than nonreligious work.
Indeed, his insistence on the priesthood of all believers meant that
a believer's everyday actions were, when carried out faithfully, right
and pleasing before God. It was actually through this work that
God was going to provide for the residents of the world. Calling
and vocation were no longer bound to the institution of the church.
Work was, for Luther, an arena in which the Christian could serve
their neighbor in service of the common good (Luther 1915).

More than that, Luther began associating the Christian's
"calling" with their profession. Drawing on a particular reading
of 1 Cor. 7:20, Luther taught that each job was itself a particular
calling, preordained by God (Weber 2001, 44). In Max Weber's
telling, this Lutheran principle meant that one lives faithfully to
God not by "not [by] surpass[ing] worldly morality in monastic
asceticism, but solely through the fulfillment of the obligations
imposed upon the individual by his position in the world. That was
his calling" (Weber 2001, 40). Labor in the world was considered
an expression of brotherly love, of divine fidelity (Weber 2001, 41).
An increased involvement in the world and one's duties lead to an
increased valuation of work, particularly as "he saw more and more
a special command of God to fulfill these particular duties which
the Divine Will had imposed upon him" (Weber 2001, 44).

Calvin refers to one's professional endeavors and everyday
works as their "calling" throughout the Institutes. Like Luther,
belief that God preordained one's riches and/or poverty was simply
downstream from belief in God's providence. Further, God called
each believer to a particular line of work, and part of the believer's
task was to prayerfully discern which professional endeavors
God was calling them toward (Calvin 2008, III.10.6). In Calvin's
perspective, work (particularly in its cursed state) played a corrective,

pedagogical role in the life of the believer, as it clarified the worker's sinful nature and lead to repentance. And this cursed experience was made sustainable by the work of Christ, who partially lifted the curse of work for God's children.

The basic hopes and commitments that drove the Reformers' treatment of work are alive and thriving in the various streams of the Faith and Work movement. Tim Keller's *Every Good Endeavor* is a helpful summation of that strategy that so many in the Faith and Work movement draw on to integrate their spiritual and professional lives. If we take Keller's text as a kind of theoretical baseline for the Faith and Work movement—and I think it's fair to do so—the movement and approach has much to commend: Keller recognizes the varied directions one's work can go; his approach is grounded in Scriptural texts and traditions; he is attentive to the nature of work as it is given by God and as it is experienced under sin; he criticizes particular ways of relating to our work (overwork, self-orientation, positioning work as the ground of our identity, etc.); he believes that the Christian tradition (and the virtues in particular) offers us resources with which we ought to navigate the challenges of our working lives; and he regularly insists that work is only ever understood as a "vocation" when it is undertaken for the common good.[2]

Problematizing That Approach

Though there is much to commend here (and in the larger Faith and Work movement), I do believe there are two primary shortcomings in this lineage, particularly as it traces itself back to the insights of the Reformers.

First, this lineage too closely associates work with vocation. Put most simply, such a reading clearly equates Martha's work with the activities of vocation. Missing altogether is any possibility that

---

[2] It is worth stressing here that I'm mostly concerning myself with one particular articulation of "vocation" in this section: that of the Faith and Work movement. There are, to be sure, countless alternative articulations of vocation that do not hinge on the collapse of vocation into professional endeavors and that do not consider contemporary capitalism as the status quo. On this front, Robert Adams' treatment of vocation in *Finite & Infinite Goods* must be commended.

Mary's prioritization of worship can and should limit or alter the category of vocation in significant ways.

It was actually Luther that began the practice of associating one's calling with one's professional endeavors, which positioned one's work not as an arena in which a faithful Christian would carry out their vocation or mission; the work itself was the vocation. This much is famously pointed out in Max Weber's famous *The Protestant Ethic and the Spirit of Capitalism*. In Weber's telling, this principle of calling, already present in Luther, was clarified and popularized in Puritanism (Calvinism, Methodism, Pietism, and Baptist life, each of which Weber treats in turn) (Weber 2001, 39).

However, collapsing vocation into work is problematic for a number of reasons. To begin with, it overestimates our work, presuming that there is some singular line of economic output to which we are ultimately called and destined. In so doing, it correlates our perception of God's hopes for our lives with our professional status, as though God is more interested in our LinkedIn connections than any relation to God or others. Articulating our vocation as a spiritual version of our work situates the tasks of discipleship within a flawed economic system. I firmly believe discipleship entails economic action (as the very nature of this book insists), but the values, practices, norms, and markers of success are distinctly different from those of contemporary capitalism.

Speaking of vocation in terms of work also overlooks a few key work-related realities. Totally absent from any such discourse are the severely raced and gendered mechanics that so intensely dictate who is placed in any particular work role. And insisting that our vocation be some successful job amid that context, this approach to vocation inadvertently correlates the benefactors of those prejudices (even if they contest the logic) with God's preference. That is, such an approach implies that the economically successful are most intensely "living into their calls and roles," even in relation to the economic exclusion and oppression of others. This is particularly problematic when we remember that wage disparities correlate to both race and sex, and they traverse nearly every major occupational category the US Bureau of Labor Statistics recognizes, prioritizing certain "workers" over and against their social, sexual, racial, and economic "others" ("Labor Force Characteristics by

Race and Ethnicity, 2019: BLS Reports: U.S. Bureau of Labor Statistics" 2019).

Further, what are we to make of unemployed persons? Does an economic downturn, outsourcing, or being laid off for any number of reasons end a person's vocation? And what does it say about our vocation when our jobs make us miserable? Or when they perpetuate injustice? Or when they don't pay us enough to survive? These are the fraught implications of presuming vocation is synonymous with work.

The second shortcoming is more fundamental. There is very little real consideration, analysis, or commentary about the structural issues that direct our working lives. This is, in my read, the most perplexing aspect of the Faith and Work movement. The authors of that Faith and Work movement draw on the reformed conviction that Christians can indeed transform systems in a way that corresponds to (even if always in a limited manner) the kingdom of God, and yet there is rarely (if ever) any real analysis about the structure of capitalism itself or the transformations needed to foster and build a more just alternative.

At its best, this vocation discourse recognizes that our public lives in pluralist shared space are part and parcel of our lives before God; there is no coherent division between the two. But at its worst, it translates to a Christianizing of whatever economic realities befall us, even while the discourse neglects to analyze or "redeem" the broader structures that animate this world. When carried out in this vein, it is simply assumed that loving God in my work can easily be carried out within the confines of how we currently work under contemporary capitalism. In so doing, the arena is assumed, its norms granted, and the proposals up for consideration are thereby limited. But I want to make the case that an Augustinian vision of vocation and the dynamics impacting ethical work require we think beyond the present norms structuring our economic lives.

Rethinking Vocation

Thankfully, Augustine's insightful read of Luke 10 offers us a constructive, alternative vision of work that does not equate one's professional endeavors with one's calling. Mary and Martha represent two distinct poles: Martha, in her tending to the necessary duties of life, represents work; Mary, in her prioritization of proximity to Christ, represents vocation. And the text urges us to distinguish between the two.

The Christian's vocation is to love God and neighbor. That can and should inform our work, but it is never reducible to our professional endeavors. And our work must be undertaken (and ultimately put down) in order to prioritize our vocation. That is, our vocation will always transcend our work and working lives. Mary's praise of Christ—her vocation—came at a cost. She put off her work duties in order to be near to Christ. Vocation displaced work, and Mary chose the better.

The passage raises a number of questions regarding the moral challenges of our work: how ought we to undertake our work in light of our vocation? When does our vocation require us to put down our work? How do we undertake our work in hopes of its eventual abolition and total displacement by our vocation? And what needs to change about our work when it is in direct tension with the demands of our vocation?

Read in this vein, I am arguing that (1) vocation is distinct from work, and (2) vocation (i.e., worship) needs to structure the ways in which we work. Worship is our vocation, and worship has significant implications regarding how we ought to work. More specifically, it should limit the work, direct the work, clarify the nature of the work, and prepare us for that work. In light of this, addressing our work-related problems is not merely an intellectual activity, as though thinking and reading can directly overcome the personal, interpersonal, and structural challenges we are facing in our current moment. Rather, liturgical labor is a mode of work one must be gracefully, prayerfully habituated into over the course of time. And our weekly liturgical gatherings of worship should play a crucial role in that process (Kaemingk and Willson 2020).

Worship of God thus attests to the ordered realities over-above the economic realm; economics, when seen from this perspective is neither all-encompassing nor soteriological. Worship thus speaks of the limits and standards against which all economic realities must be measured and held accountable (Bretherton 2009, 97). When read in relation to the broader economic theology I am developing here, worship functions as a standard for just economic relations, agencies, and forms of exchange. One cannot love God apart from a proper use of oneself and relation to one's neighbors in the world. I am thus framing vocation as the conceptual rubric through which we can evaluate the justice and proper placement of work in the life of the Christian.

Most specifically, this reimagined understanding of vocation (i.e., worship as "enjoyment of God," if we are to stick with Augustine's terminology) offers us the contours through which we might begin imagining a Christian vision of work: worship limits work, directs work, clarifies work, and prepares us for work.

The category of vocation-as-worship contests our drive toward overwork. Augustine writes, "No one ought to be so completely at leisure that in his leisure he takes no thought for serving his neighbor, nor should anyone be so fully active that he makes no room for the contemplation of God" (*civ. Dei.* XIV.19). It is not, in fact, the activities of work or leisure themselves that are to be properly enjoyed; those modes of agency, important as they might be for our life during the world, are only to be used in God so as to make possible our enjoyment of God (*civ. Dei.* XIV.19). To a certain extent, worship—particularly when articulated in this Augustinian register—insists that humans are created for nonproductive ends. We are created to delight in God, for God's delight first and foremost, which is simultaneously our own derivative delight as well (Mathewes 2004, 214; Williams 2016c). Worship thus brackets work in insisting that work has no meaning apart from its reference to God; work must come to an end in order to make space and time for more formative pursuits. That cluster of insights is a direct challenge to contemporary productivism and the contemporary work ethics this project aims to problematize.

Vocation-as-worship also directs work. Augustine, perhaps unsurprisingly, insists that work and the products of our work are not all that valuable in and of themselves. Their real value is only perceived and taken advantage of when they are properly directed toward their ends: love of God and neighbor. From this vantage point, our relation to our work and the products of our work matters a great deal. What ought to be prized is the sake for which we undertake that work and the ways in which we let those motivating factors animate our work. For Augustine, to work "rightfully and helpfully" is to work to "contribut[e] to the well-being of those set around us" (*civ. Dei.* XIV.19). Work, undertaken in the love of God, must be undertaken for the common good. He thus concludes, "It is the love of truth, then, that seeks holy leisure, and it is the drive of love that takes on righteous activity" (*civ. Dei.* XIV.19).

Vocation-as-worship clarifies work as well. The very act of worshipping God is only ever made possible by the transformation of our wills enabled by the grace of Christ. This gets interesting when we realize that agents' rediscovery of their freedom depends on a "reintegration of their affective structure, through their loves' conversion back to congruity with their natural desires" (Mathewes 1999, 208). As such, a properly Christian vision of work—working in freedom—depends on a properly reintegrated vision of one's affective structure made possible by a life of love wherein we grow into God during the *saeculum*. To grow into this vision of work is thus to grow into Christ and the virtues Christ enables.

Relatedly, vocation-as-worship prepares us for work. That is, worship forms our imaginations regarding how to work and how to engage with the structures that make possible (and demand) our work. The ongoing formation made possible through an attentive participation in the liturgical year has profound implications for Christian political witness. The Christian political imagination is, at its best, nurtured and cultivated in relation to the spatial and temporal ordering of the liturgy (Bretherton 2009, 192–3). So, in addition to worship being the standard by which the justice and proper use of any economic agency or structure is to be evaluated, worship is also the means through which just practices and alternatives can come to be envisioned. When considered in this register, worship becomes the means through which I find a sustainable middle ground between Martha's productive undertakings and Mary's nonproductive praise.

New Work Structures, New Ways of Working (A Conclusion)

My framing of worship and its work-related implications of Augustine's reading of Luke 10 have largely focused on individual practices and formation thus far. But it must be stressed that mine is not an individualistic proposal alone, as though praying, going to church, and virtuous formation necessarily make one's work life and work relations faithful, joyful, meaningful, healthy, or ethical. There are structural and cultural realities—realities outside the control of any one individual—that foster unhealthy modes of work, attachment, and relations. To be clear, thinking extensively about the vision of work I have developed here (along with Augustine's notion of attachment and neighbor-love) requires we think systematically about our economic structures, even if such a gesture goes beyond Augustine's own tendencies. Put differently, I believe Augustine's vision of work and his understanding of attachment requires we rethink some of those basic structures so as to create more potential for working faithfully.

Additionally, avoiding any structural analysis runs the risk of justifying the sinful, unjust practices of our present economic order. I am not proposing a vision of work that is impossible, utopic, or other-worldly. To do so would be to ultimately legitimate the present order and norms, which is precisely what I mean to contest. In order to demonstrate some of the structural issues that must be altered and the viability of such shifts in the here and now (yes, even amid millennial capitalism and a neoliberal order), I will conclude the chapter with a brief examination of one particular type of cooperative business structure: the worker self-directed enterprise. Doing so, I believe clarifies one viable means through which the most practical implications of the Lukan passage can be carried out.

Contexts capable of fostering the kind of work I have sketched here are more frequent than one might initially suspect. Consider how common the cooperative enterprise already is. As Nathan Schneider has explained in his recent *Everything for Everyone*,

> [t]he International cooperative Alliance calculates that the largest cooperatives globally generate about $2.2 trillion in turnover and employ about 12 percent of the employed population in G20 countries. As much as 10 percent of the world's total employment happens through co-ops. According to the United Nations the world's 2.6 million co-ops count over 1 billion members and clients among them, plus $20 trillion in assets, with revenue that adds up to 4.3 percent of the global GDP. (Schneider 2018, 10–11)

But if a co-op is a general, catchall term for communally owned, democratically operated businesses, let us consider one particular model in closing: the worker self-directed enterprise (WSDE, henceforth). Economist Richard Wolff sets out to define WSDEs by demonstrating their differences from contemporary private capitalism's norm of corporations (Wolff 2012, 117). In corporations, shareholders typically vote to determine how the company's board of directors is composed. Very rarely are those boards composed of workers from within the corporation. The corporate board, once established, is in charge of appropriating and distributing the company's surplus profit, and they also determine the contents and rate of production. The board of a WSDE, on the other hand, is solely composed of the productive members of its enterprise. "All of the workers who produce the surplus generated inside the enterprise function collectively to appropriate and distribute it. They alone compose the board of directors" (Wolff 2012, 118). Hence, they are "self-directed." Within this framework, it is the workers themselves who determine what is produced, how much is produced, the technology used in that production process, and the various other details bound up in the maintenance of that central vision. This is what distinguishes the WSDE from standard business models of late-capitalism, in both their state and private forms: the workers who produce surpluses in WSDEs are the same people that use and distribute them (Wolff 2012, 118–19).

WSDEs are also characterized by their democratic nature, which determines how and where the enterprise's surpluses are distributed. That is, each productive worker's role entails both standard production and service as an equal member of the enterprise's board, which makes its decisions through a democratic decision-making process. That board would, for example, collectively determine to pay taxes, set budgets for departments, negotiate salaries, and determine what to do with the surplus. Such a process will, by definition, require collaboration and compromise given the number of people in the room and the multiplicity of commitments represented therein (Wolff 2012, 125). WSDEs are therefore characterized by two principles: "that the appropriation and distribution of the surplus are done cooperatively and that the workers who cooperatively produce the surplus and those who cooperatively appropriate and distribute it are identical."

Wolff argues that WSDEs fit Marx's technical definition for "nonexploitative institutions" because the surplus produced is never appropriated by anyone outside that party (Wolff 2012, 122–3).

The cooperative enterprise (and the WSDE) can provide opportunities for liturgical labor because of the way it reimagines basic business structures and labor practices, thereby fostering more properly ordered relations to and in labor. That is, the WSDE can, under the right conditions, make available a form of economic agency that corresponds to Augustine's understanding of "use," wherein inhabitants of the city of God are freed to "use" the fruits of their capacities in and for the sake of their enjoyment of God (doc. Chr. 1.3.3).

Within the confines of the WSDE, for example, the board is in charge of setting production goals and schedules, and so the workers themselves get to determine their commitments to rest, vacation, and leisure time. They are thus capable of constructing their own work/rest balance. They know the cost of sustaining the production and involved parties, and they can set their hours accordingly in order to meet or exceed those needs. Absent any external demand for hyper-productivity, workers are free to enter into a new relation to their own productive capacities and activities. WSDEs thereby enable alternative modes of production that do not require the manipulative time-management and work-ethic discourses perpetuated in typical capitalist labor structures. Such possibilities could, over time, bring some actual shifts to the culture of overwork that capitalism has helped to foster (Wolff 2012, 133).

This process should also help to reduce the income disparities that have grown so high in recent years. Within this model, salaries are negotiated by the board, which is itself the collection of workers. This shared information and the inevitable negotiations that information leads to would be more likely to reduce unjust gaps in pay. Some WSDEs might even institute minimum and maximum salaries. If we begin to read the cultivation of balanced working lives, the prioritization of communal concerns, and the financial empowerment of our coworkers as concrete forms of loving one's neighbor (and I believe these are some of the most concrete ways in which I can love my neighbor as myself), then the WSDE presents workers with an opportunity to love God in and through their love of neighbor, with the latter being actively played out (at least partially) in a practical, economic manner.

It must be stressed, though, that the point of this excursus on the WSDE is not to imply that this unique business model is somehow more graced than a standard corporation, as though God's grace could be only released and effective in the wake of certain transformations in business structure. Rather, my aim is to suggest that grace informs, underlies, and inspires the Christian's attempt to improve labor relations and conditions. If, as I suggested earlier, "liturgical labor" is a mode of labor funded by the transformative power of grace—wherein the self's loves are redirected to foster the proper use of others, the world, and the self—then grace itself should be driving our interest in structures like the WSDE, to the extent that these structures are capable of fostering more just labor relations.

I imagine there will be a wide range of criticisms, anxieties, and questions at this point. Some secular non-Christians might worry I am calling for some kind of Christian overtaking of a non-Christian business model. And some Christians might worry that I am prioritizing a secular business structure as the site of grace over and against that of the church itself. But both of those concerns misunderstand my claims here, and once again, I think Augustine's sense of the pagan virtues can help us think through my positioning of the WSDE. As I established in chapter four, Augustine acknowledges the church remains indistinguishable from the earthly city during the *saeculum*. This matters because it is certainly possible that a virtuous Christian experiencing transformation through grace can take on certain kinds of temporal, relational, and formational dynamics in their labor that are largely indistinguishable from those of non-Christians (Tornau 2019, 7.2).

Such an insight should structure readers' perception of my treatment of the WSDE. I am not claiming that the WSDE is some inherently Christian business structure, and I am not claiming it is a necessarily graced or graceful entity. Nor am I suggesting the potential of liturgical labor can or will occur outside of the church or a life of virtuous formation enabled by God's grace. I also do not mean to suggest that the WSDE is an incoherent undertaking outside the parameters of Christian theology and formation; remember: a virtuous Christian's interest in the labor dynamics potentially fostered in the WSDE will be largely indistinguishable from their non-Christian colleagues.

I have been arguing that the Christian's virtuous formation and growth into Christ need to impact and influence their conception of work, the way they undertake their work, and the way they relate to their coworkers and the objects of their labor. And virtuous Christians should actively seek ways to let their love of God, the world, and their neighbors impact and direct their working lives. Hence my interest in analyzing the WSDE. My aim has been to highlight the structure's different use and conception of labor precisely because I believe this structure is capable of fostering a healthier, more just set of labor dynamics than alternative business models under capitalism.

Lastly, none of this is to suggest that the potential of the monastic context and virtuously informed "liturgical labor" easily translates into contemporary capitalism and everyday labor experiences. Quite the opposite, in fact. The extent to which there is any potential for spiritual and moral reformation in labor largely depends on properly navigating labor relations (to labor, to those we labor with, to ourselves in labor, to the objects of our labor). But when properly related to and carried out, this mode of labor has the potential to become a modality of prayer, thereby radically transforming our laboring lives and selves, even in a time such as this.

Drawing on Augustine's reading of Mary and Martha's competing agencies in Luke 10, I have attempted in this chapter to characterize work as a distinctly human, sinful phenomenon that must be endured during our lives in the world, even as we hope for its eventual abolition in the eschaton. Such an approach, I argued, clarifies some of the problems with our current understanding of and relation to work while also implicitly prescribing some constructive alternatives. And so this treatment of the WSDE only matters to the extent that I believe it represents some practical, viable, structural possibilities in which Christians can undertake the necessary work of today in ways that are animated by a critical awareness of work's coming abolition.

Conclusion

Or "What Just Happened?"

In this conclusion I aim to accomplish three tasks: (1) remind readers of the problem to which this work is responding—which is to say rearticulate the *why* of this project; (2) summarize (and review) the argument that has just been given; and (3) sketch something of the research agenda precipitated by this project.

The Problem and the Why

I began this project by arguing that our work-related problems are both economic and cultural in nature.

On the economic front, pensions are falling, huge numbers of low-wage workers lack employer-provided health coverage, and the US Department of Labor continues recovering record amounts of back and stolen wages from employers. For those fortunate enough to have consistent jobs, life consists of labor and recovery. From 2000 to 2012, workplace productivity increased by 23 percent, while real wages increased by less than 1 percent (Ho 2009, 16). According to the Economic Policy Institute, "[s]ince 1979, productivity has risen six times faster than hourly compensation for the typical U.S. worker" ("Job Growth Stays Solid but Wages Disappoint—Again" 2019). The effects of such forms of wage depression are similar to those of unemployment. When laborers are denied benefits and enough hours to make ends meet, taxpayers inevitably pick up the costs of those medical bills and forms of necessary social assistance.

Our labor opportunities and associated incomes are, additionally, intensely gendered and racialized. Women are more likely than men to be counted among the working poor, and Blacks and Latinos alike are more likely to be counted among that group than their white counterparts ("A Profile of the Working Poor, 2018: BLS Reports: U.S. Bureau of Labor Statistics" 2018). Wage disparities correlate to both race and sex, and they traverse nearly every major occupational category the US Bureau of Labor Statistics recognizes ("Labor Force Characteristics by Race and Ethnicity, 2019: BLS Reports: U.S. Bureau of Labor Statistics" 2019). The troubling history of reproductive labor corroborates these trends, highlighting the long history we have of distributing labor according to perceived racial and gender hierarchies.

The difficulty of living on such wages is further compounded when laborers do not receive the full payments contractually owed them, which is shockingly common. Wage theft is a new norm through which some employers discipline and control their labor force. To highlight the magnitude of this problem, the Economic Policy Institute projected the total value of material property stolen in the States in 2012 to be $340 million. The amount recovered from wage theft (i.e., not the total amount stolen) in the same time period was $933 million (Meixell and Eisenbrey 2014).

But the issues do not stop there; they are not easily contained within a fictitious economic boundary; they have taken hold of our imaginations and hearts as well. We have totally misunderstood the possibilities and nature of work. We work more than most developed countries, we take fewer vacations, and we tend to retire later. Our drive for work is more emotional, cultural, and spiritual than it is economic.

This makes some sense when we note the intense ways our working lives have come to stand in for our personal successes and meaning. We experience constant pressures at work to be more efficient and productive, and we know the ways in which our work structures contribute to a seemingly ever-growing, corrosive system of poverty and oppression. And yet we continue working at alarming rates. Studies show that the majority of Americans hate their work, and yet we continue working at dangerous rates given our deeply engrained work ethics.

We must reckon with the economic and cultural aspects of these problems alike, and we must do so in tandem. There can be no redress to the structural inequalities stemming from our everyday work and the new norms of wage theft and wage discrimination if we do not also reckon with our problematic work ethics and tendencies toward productivity. Our work will neither save us, but the effects of our misunderstandings of work will indeed kill us.

The Argument

Against that backdrop, I argued that St. Augustine's theological system contains a trove of rich resources and ideas through which we could piece together an alternative theology of work. Systematizing and unifying those insights so as to offer a counter-vision of work has been the primary aim of this project.

In examining a few of his letters, I demonstrated his use of "work" as a metaphor for sanctification in the life of the believer. Our growth into God is itself a kind of work made possible by grace; putting on Christ is toilsome given the ways we have chained ourselves to sinful habits, but we are to undertake that work in hope of the rest that is to come. These are good works, full of toil, aimed at rest. In that little metaphorical usage of "work" rests an entire theology of work. And so in the remainder of the first chapter, we began charting the nature and meaning of work in relation to the final end. In exploring his treatment of the soul in De Quantitate Animae and his theological anthropology we found the ends for which the human was created, which Augustine believed can and should inform the way we work. Work's nature and meaning, it turns out, are only legible in relation to the human being's purpose, nature, and place within the order of creation. In the end, I argued that the Augustinian task facing the believer hoping to work faithfully is to orient and undertake their work in service of the flourishing of their inner needs: knowing, loving, and resting in God.

In the second chapter, I explore his Genesis commentaries to make sense of his treatments of the nature of work in Eden. Work, it turns out, is not a result of the fall; it was built into the heart of creation. And in the garden of Eden—whatever we mean when we say "the garden of Eden"—work was no hardship. According to Augustine, it was some kind of mysterious, spontaneous experience of joy grounded in human agency rightly ordered according to God's love and the human's place in a complexly ordered, created system. Examining that work further clarified the ends for which work was created and the confluence of agencies (divine and human) that make work possible. God—being closer to me than I am myself, being that Being in whom we move and live and have our freedom—exhibits a form of action that is the source and empowerment of our own agency. God is thus more intimate to our working selves and lives than we are.

In Augustine's theology of sin, I found the implications regarding the limits and risks of working in a sinful world. Because the entrance of sin entails the deformation and disordering of our minds and wills, sin is more an issue of the sinner's disposition than anything else. In sin, we love the world, ourselves, our work, and the objects of our labor disproportionally and for ourselves apart from God and neighbor. And in so doing, we overestimate what we are capable of in our work, and we selfishly privatize what is to be shared by God through us. The good news, though, is that these are depths of human being that Christ entered into so as to gracefully redeem our disordered minds and wills. And in the wake of that redemptive process, we have the potential to act faithfully amid a sinful world. And so, at the end of third chapter, I charted in Augustine's infamous use/enjoyment dyad the resources through which we can articulate a faithful navigation of work amid our sinful world. We are to use ourselves (working capacities included) for the sake of enjoying God.

Using oneself for the enjoyment of God is quite vague, though. In order to clarify what's at stake in such a vision, I turned to Augustine's treatment of work within the monastic life as it is articulated in *De Opere Monachorum*. In that little text on the labor strike at a monastery, we discovered something of a positive vision of labor properly oriented toward a love of God. Through a constructive read of that strange text, I argued that labor, when grounded in a life of liturgy and virtue, can be transformed such that it's undertaken anew, even if a world dominated by global capital. Grace-enabled labor has the potential to sharpen one's love of God and prepare one for further transformation into the life of God.

In Augustine's sermons and commentaries on the New Testament, I found his articulation of the eventual abolition of work in the eschaton. In the fifth chapter I turned to his constructive read of Luke 10, he articulates the tensions of working faithfully in a sinful world. We are stuck carrying out the necessary, mundane tasks of work (as is represented by Martha) in hopes of a coming future where productive activity will be overcome by blissful rest in God (as is represented by Mary). And Jesus' response to Martha—"Mary chose the better"—has some profound implications regarding our own cultural obsessions with productive output. We need to figure out how to put down work in order to take a larger share in what's already been given to us: God itself.

The kind of grace-enabled transformation I have been gesturing toward (what I've previously called "liturgical labor") depends on a reordering of our relation to God, ourselves, our work, the objects of our labor, and the folks we work with. Because that vision runs the risk of sounding unrealist, other-worldly, or utopic, I've sketched one brief model I believe resonates with the vision of labor here: the worker self-directed enterprise. This is not to say such a business model is itself graced or the only logical possibility; it is to demonstrate the present, ongoing, historic, and economic viability of carrying out our labor and labor relations in transformed ways. These are the systems and modes of work I believe believers should be striving for imagining, building, and undertaking.

At its most simple, this project is predicated on the reality of an economy that overemphasizes and exploits our working capacities and identities. Within that context, work offers us unique opportunities for either disintegration or prayerful formation into the life of God. In light of that context, the basic thesis of this book has been that work is a uniquely human phenomenon which must be endured, properly related to, and thereby directed toward the love of God, even as we await (in hope) that day when contemplation of God displaces and abolishes productive agency altogether.

Where to From Here?

This project has been an attempt to begin filling the void of economic analysis that structures so much of political Augustinianism. Without an adequate analysis of the crucial role that capitalism plays in structuring contemporary politics and American life, we severely misrepresent the nuanced mechanics, pressures, and needs for structuring a faithfully Christian sketch of public life. This economic reading of Augustine has much to offer Augustinian studies and conversations regarding economic justice among religiously minded folks. I have here only focused on the particular topic of work. But much more can and should be on the matter.

Augustine's *City of God* gives us pieces of a political-theological ethic that has profound economic implications regarding engagement with the economic structures that so vividly animate our contemporary world. Within the context of contemporary capitalism, faithful economic life should be characterized by community organizing and theologically motivated economic acts, through which those aspiring to be counted among the city of God seek to foster earthly peace and make use of the city's temporal goods in hope and love for all. According to this Augustinian vision, there can be no finished, final form of economic life—hence his understanding of the import of criticizing idolatrous political (and economic) systems. The task of faithful life in the midst of structures and systems marked by the drive for self-possession and domination is to foster virtue and peace to whatever extent possible. Faithful economic witness must critically name (and thereby delimit) the ideologies of domination and lust that characterize contemporary capitalism and seek to foster peace within the necessarily limited conditions of the *saeculum*. The city of God should function according to an economic vision altogether distinct from the norms of contemporary capitalism, even within the structures and culture of contemporary capitalism itself.

The church is, according to Augustine, properly constituted as a *res publica*—a commonwealth—in and through its worship of God. As such, it should stand in stark contrast to the ideologies and assumptions of the city of mammon, driven as it is by market dynamics and productivist work ethics (Bretherton 2009, 143). The church's worship clarifies its mode of social engagement, freeing the church to attest that the world (like our neighbors) is not ours for consumption. It is, rather, a good gift of God that is continually dependent on God and given in grace and love to enable our communion with God.

If that is right (and I believe it is), then much more must be said on the matter. And the good news is that I believe there are many more rich resources lying dormant in Augustine's system with which to ponder these things. A systematic treatment of Augustine and economy would need to (1) further lay bare the bankrupt economic assumptions animating our present, (2) further develop the methodology briefly alluded to here, and (3) theologize the church's economic engagement. Then the Augustinian analysis and theology could be extended to treatments of property and wealth alike, in addition to work.

It is to this task I must now turn.

REFERENCES

"A Profile of the Working Poor, 2018: BLS Reports: US Bureau of Labor Statistics." (2018). Available online: https://www.bls.gov/opub/reports/working-poor/2018/home.htm (accessed December 15, 2020).

Arbesmann, Rudolph (1973). "The Attitude of St. Augustine Toward Labor." In David Neiman and Margaret Schatkin (eds), *The Heritage of the Early Church: Essays in Honor of the Very Reverend Georges Vasilievich Florovsky*, 245–459. Rome: Pont. Institutum Studiorum Orientalium.

Augustine (1933). *De Quantitate Animae*. Trans. Francis E. Tourscher. Philadelphia: The Peter Reilly Company.

Augustine (1937). *De Libero Arbitrio*. Trans. Francis E. Tourscher. Philadelphia: The Peter Reilly Company.

Augustine (1992). *Sermons Volume 4: 94A–147A*. Ed. John E. Rotelle. Trans. O. P. Edmund Hill. Vol. III/4 (94A–147A). Brooklyn: New City Press.

Augustine (1995). "Contra Priscillianistas." In Roland J. Teske S.J. (trans.), *Arianism and Other Heresies, Vol. I.18. The Works of Saint Augustine: A Translation for the 21st Century*, 104–18. Hyde Park: New City Press.

Augustine (1996). *De Doctrina Christiana*. Trans. Edmund Hill. 2nd Revised ed. (Vol. I/11, The Works of Saint Augustine: A Translation for the 21st Century). Brooklyn: New City Press.

Augustine (1997a). "De Peccatorum Meritis et Remissione et de Baptism Parvulorum." In *Answer to the Pelagians 1*, 19–134 (Vol. I/23, The Works of Saint Augustine: A Translation for the 21st Century), Introductions, translations, and notes by Roland J. Teske, S.J. Hyde Park: New City Press.

Augustine (1997b). *Letters 1–99*. (Vol. II/1, The Works of Saint Augustine: A Translation for the 21st Century). Brooklyn: New City Press.

Augustine (2000). *Enarrationes in Psalmos*. 1st ed. (Vol. 1, The Works of Saint Augustine: A Translation for the 21st Century). Hyde Park: New City Press.

Augustine (2001). *Confessiones*. Trans. Maria Boulding. Hyde Park: New City Press.

Augustine (2002a). *De Opere Monachorum*. 1st pbk. reprint. (Fathers of the Church). Washington: Catholic University of America Press.

Augustine (2002b). *Letters 100–155*. (Vol. II/2, The Works of Saint Augustine: A Translation for the 21st Century). Brooklyn: New City Press.

Augustine (2004a). "*De Genesi Ad Litteram*." In *On Genesis*, 155–506 (The Works of Saint Augustine: A Translation for the 21st Century), Introductions, translations, and notes by Edmund Hill, O.P. Hyde Park: New City Press.

Augustine (2004b). "*De Genesi Ad Litteram Liber Imperfectus*." In *On Genesis*, 105–54 (The Works of Saint Augustine: A Translation for the 21st Century), Introductions, translations, and notes by Edmund Hill, O.P. Hyde Park: New City Press.

Augustine (2004c). "*De Genesi Adversus Manichaeos*." In *On Genesis*, 25–104 (The Works of Saint Augustine: A Translation for the 21st Century), Introductions, translations, and notes by Edmund Hill, O.P. Hyde Park: New City Press.

Augustine (2008a). *De Diversas Quaestionibus Octoginta Tribus*. (Vol. 1/12, The Works of Saint Augustine: A Translation for the 21st Century). Hyde Park: New City Press.

Augustine (2008b). *In Epistulam Johannis Ad Parthos Tractatus*. Trans. Boniface Ramsey (Vol. III/14, Works of Saint Augustine). Hyde Park: New City Press.

Augustine (2012a). *De Trinitate*. Trans. O. P. Edmund Hill. 2nd ed. (Vol. I/5, The Works of Saint Augustine: A Translation for the 21st Century). Hyde Park: New City Press.

Augustine (2012b). *De Civitate Dei*. 1st ed. Vol. 2. 2 vols. Hyde Park: New City Press.

Augustine (2012c). *De Civitate Dei*. Trans. William S. Babcock (Vol. 1. 2 vols, The Works of Saint Augustine: A Translation for the 21st Century, I/6). Hyde Park: New City Press.

Barsella, Susanna (2014). "Ars and Theology: Work, Salvation, and Social Doctrine in the Early Church Fathers." *Annali d'Italianistica* 32: 53–73.

Bauman, Zygmunt (2000). *Liquid Modernity*. Malden: Polity.

Berry, Wendell (2010). "Economy and Pleasure." In *What Matters?: Economics for a Renewed Commonwealth*, 2nd ed., 89–104. Berkeley: Counterpoint.

Berry, Wendell (2019a). "The Total Economy." In *What I Stand On: The Collected Essays of Wendell Berry 1969–2017*, Vol. 2, 280–94. New York: Library of America.

Berry, Wendell (2019b). "Two Economies." In *What I Stand On: The Collected Essays of Wendell Berry 1969–2017*, Vol. 1, 600–18. New York: Library of America.

Bertino, John (2017). "Five Things Millennial Workers Want More Than A Fat Paycheck." *Forbes*. Available online: https://www.forbes.com/ sites/forbescoachescouncil/2017/10/26/five-things-millennial-workers -want-more-than-a-fat-paycheck/ (accessed April 3, 2019).

Bretherton, Luke (2009). *Christianity and Contemporary Politics: The Conditions and Possibilities of Faithful Witness*. Malden: Wiley-Blackwell.

Brockwell, Charles W. (1977). "Augustine's Ideal of Monastic Community: A Paradigm for His Doctrine of the Church." *Augustinian Studies* 8: 91–109.

Brown, Peter (2012). *Through the Eye of a Needle: Wealth, The Fall of Rome, and the Making of Christianity in the West, 350–550 AD*. Princeton: Princeton University Press.

Brown, Peter (2013). *Augustine of Hippo: A Biography*. 1st ed., Forty-Fifth Anniversary ed. Berkeley; New York: University of California Press.

Brown, Wendy (2017). *Undoing the Demos: Neoliberalism's Stealth Revolution*. Brooklyn: Zone Books.

Calvin, John (2008). *Institutes of the Christian Religion*. Revised ed. Peabody: Hendrickson Publishers.

Cavanaugh, William T., and James K. A. Smith (2017). "Introduction: Beyond Galileo to Chalcedon." In William T. Cavanaugh and James K. A. Smith (eds), *Evolution and the Fall*, xv–1. Grand Rapids: Wm. B. Eerdmans Publishing Co.

Clavier, Mark (2018). *On Consumer Culture, Identity, The Church and the Rhetorics of Delight*. London: Bloomsbury Academic.

Cohen, Lizabeth (2003). *A Consumers' Republic: The Politics of Mass Consumption in Postwar America*. New York: Vintage Books.

Cooper, David and Teresa Kroeger (2017). *Employers Steal Billions from Workers' Paychecks Each Year: Survey Data Show Millions of Workers Are Paid Less than the Minimum Wage, at Significant Cost to Taxpayers and State Economies*. Washington, DC: Economic Policy Institute.

Dodaro, Robert (2004). "Political and Theological Virtues in Augustine, Letter 155 to Macedonius." *Augustiniana* 54 (1/4): 431–74.

Dodaro, Robert (2008). *Christ and the Just Society in the Thought of Augustine*. Cambridge: Cambridge University Press.

Ernst, Allie M. (2009). *Martha from the Margins the Authority of Martha in Early Christian Tradition*. Supplements to Vigiliae Christianae, v. 98. Leiden: Brill.

Falk, Derrel R. (2017). "Human Origins: The Scientific Story." In William T. Cavanaugh and James K. A. Smith (eds), *Evolution and the Fall*, 2–22. Grand Rapids: Wm. B. Eerdmans Publishing Co.

Gaul, Brett (2009). "Augustine on the Virtues of the Pagans." *Augustinian Studies* 40 (2): 233–49. https://doi.org/10.5840/augstudies200940223.

Graeber, David (2019). *Bullshit Jobs: A Theory*. Reprint ed. New York: Simon & Schuster.

Gregory, Eric (2010). *Politics and the Order of Love: An Augustinian Ethic of Democratic Citizenship*. Chicago: University of Chicago Press.

Griffith, Erin (2019). "Why Are Young People Pretending to Love Work?" *The New York Times*, February 22, 2019, sec. Business. Available online: https://www.nytimes.com/2019/01/26/business/against-hustle -culture-rise-and-grind-tgim.html.

Griffiths, Paul (2012). "Secularity and the Saeculum." In James Wetzel (ed.), *Augustine's City of God: A Critical Guide*, 14–32. Cambridge: Cambridge University Press.

Grote, Andreas E. J. (2013). "De Opere Monachorum." In Karla Pollmann and Willemien Otten (eds), David Gascoigne (trans.), *The Oxford Guide to the Historical Reception of Augustine*, 1st ed., 360–3. Oxford: Oxford University Press.

Hadot, Pierre (2002). *What Is Ancient Philosophy?* Trans. Michael Chase. Cambridge: Belknap Press.

Harding, Brian (2008). *Augustine and Roman Virtue*. 1st ed. London; New York: Continuum.

Hardoon, Deborah (2017). *An Economy for the 99%*. Briefing Paper. Oxford: Oxfam.

Hill, Edmund (2004). "General Introduction." In *On Genesis*, 13–35 (The Works of Saint Augustine: A Translation for the 21st Century), Introductions, translations, and notes by Edmund Hill. O.P. Hyde Park: New City Press.

Hill, Edmund (2012). "Foreword to Books IX–XIV." In Edmund Hill (trans.), *The Trinity*, 2nd ed., 323–36. New City Press.

Ho, Karen (2009). *Liquidated: An Ethnography of Wall Street*. Durham: Duke University Press Books.

Hollingworth, Miles (2013). *Saint Augustine of Hippo: An Intellectual Biography*. 1st ed. New York: Oxford University Press.

"Job Growth Stays Solid but Wages Disappoint—Again." (2019). *Economic Policy Institute* (blog). Available online: https://www.epi.org /press/job-growth-stays-solid-but-wages-disappoint-again/ (accessed December 15, 2020).

Kaemingk, Matthew and Cory B. Willson (2020). *Work and Worship: Reconnecting Our Labor and Liturgy*. Grand Rapids: Baker Academic.

Keynes, John Maynard (2012). "Economic Possibilities for Our
  Grandchildren." In *Essays in Persuasion*, 358–73. New York: Martino
  Fine Books.
Kidwell, Jeremy H. (2013). "Labour in Augustine's Thought." In Karla
  Pollmann and Willemien Otten (eds), *The Oxford Guide to the
  Historical Reception of Augustine*, 779–84. Oxford: Oxford University
  Press.
Knotts, Matthew W. (2019). *On Creation, Science, Disenchantment
  and the Contours of Being and Knowing*. New York: Bloomsbury
  Academic & Professional. Available online: http://ebookcentral
  .proquest.com/lib/vand/detail.action?docID=5825190.
"Labor Force Characteristics by Race and Ethnicity, 2019: BLS Reports:
  US Bureau of Labor Statistics." (2019). Available online: https://www
  .bls.gov/opub/reports/race-and-ethnicity/2019/home.htm (accessed
  December 15, 2020).
Lofton, Kathryn (2017). *Consuming Religion*. 1st ed. Chicago: University
  of Chicago Press.
Luther, Martin (1915). "An Open Letter to the Christian Nobility."
  In C. M. Jacobs (trans.), *Works of Martin Luther*, 48–116, Vol. II.
  Philadelphia: A. J. Holman Company.
Luther, Martin (2012). *Treatise on Good Works: Luther Study Edition*.
  Luther study ed. Minneapolis: Fortress Press.
Mann, William E. (2014). "Augustine on Evil and Original Sin." In
  David Vincent Meconi and Eleonore Stump (eds), *The Cambridge
  Companion to Augustine*, 2nd ed., 98–107. Cambridge: Cambridge
  University Press.
Mathewes, Charles (1999). "Augustinian Anthropology: Interior Intimo
  Meo." *The Journal of Religious Ethics* 27 (2): 195–221.
Mathewes, Charles (2003). "Book One: The Presumptuousness of
  Autobiography and the Paradoxes of Beginning." In Kim Paffenroth
  and Robert Peter Kennedy (eds), *A Reader's Companion to
  Augustine's Confessions*, 1st ed., 7–23. Louisville: Westminster John
  Knox Press.
Mathewes, Charles (2004). "On Using the World." In William Schweiker
  and Charles Mathewes (eds), *Having: Property and Possession in
  Religious and Social Life*, 189–221. Grand Rapids: Eerdmans Pub Co.
Mathewes, Charles (2008). *A Theology of Public Life*. Cambridge:
  Cambridge University Press.
Mathewes, Charles (2010). *The Republic of Grace: Augustinian Thoughts
  for Dark Times*. Grand Rapids: Eerdmans.
Meixell, Brady, and Ross Eisenbrey (2014). "An Epidemic of Wage Theft
  Is Costing Workers Hundreds of Millions of Dollars a Year." *Economic
  Policy Institute* (blog). Available online: http://www.epi.org/publication

/epidemic-wage-theft-costing-workers-hundreds/ (accessed October 28, 2016).

Moore, Karl (2014). "Millennials Work For Purpose, Not Paycheck." *Forbes*. Available online: https://www.forbes.com/sites/karlmoore/2014/10/02/millennials-work-for-purpose-not-paycheck/ (accessed April 3, 2019).

Niederbacher, Bruno, S.J. (2014). "The Human Soul: Augustine's Case for Soul-Body Dualism." In David Vincent Meconi and Eleonore Stump (eds), *The Cambridge Companion to Augustine*, 2nd ed., 125–41. Cambridge: Cambridge University Press.

Ochs, Peter (2002). "Talmudic Scholarship as Textual Reasoning: Halvini's Pragmatic Historiography." In Peter Ochs and Nance Leven (eds), *Textual Readings: Jewish Philosophy and Text Study at the End of the Twentieth Century*, 120–43. Grand Rapids: Eerdmans.

Ochs, Peter (2011). *Another Reformation: Postliberal Christianity and the Jews*. Grand Rapids: Baker Academic.

O'Donovan, Oliver (2003). "The Political Thought of City of God 19." In Joan Lockwood O'Donovan and Oliver O'Donovan (eds), *Bonds of Imperfection*, 48–72. Grand Rapids: Eerdmans.

O'Donovan, Oliver (2017). *Entering into Rest* (Ethics as Theology 3). Grand Rapids: William B. Eerdmans Publishing Company.

Rist, John (1997). *Augustine: Ancient Thought Baptized*. Cambridge: Cambridge University Press.

Sandel, Michael J. (2012). *What Money Can't Buy: The Moral Limits of Markets*. 1st ed. New York: Farrar, Straus and Giroux.

Schneider, Nathan (2018). *Everything for Everyone: The Radical Tradition That Is Shaping the Next Economy*. 1st ed. New York: Bold Type Books.

Schuurman, Douglas J. (2003). *Vocation: Discerning Our Callings in Life*. Grand Rapids: Eerdmans.

Smith, James K. A. (2017). "What Stands on the Fall? A Philosophical Exploration." In William T. Cavanaugh and James K. A. Smith (eds), *Evolution and the Fall*, 48–64. Grand Rapids: Wm. B. Eerdmans Publishing Co.

Stock, Brian (1996). *Augustine the Reader: Meditation, Self-Knowledge, and the Ethics of Interpretation*. Cambridge: Harvard University Press.

Tanner, Kathryn (2004). *God and Creation in Christian Theology*. Minneapolis: Augsburg Fortress Publishers.

Tanner, Kathryn (2019). *Christianity and the New Spirit of Capitalism*. New Haven: Yale University Press.

Taylor, Charles (2018). *A Secular Age*. Reprint ed. Cambridge; London: Belknap Press; An Imprint of Harvard University Press.

Thompson, Derek (2019). "Workism Is Making Americans Miserable." *The Atlantic*, February 24, 2019. Available online: https://www

.theatlantic.com/ideas/archive/2019/02/religion-workism-making
-americans-miserable/583441/.

Tornau, Christian (2019). "Saint Augustine." In Edward N. Zalta (ed.),
The Stanford Encyclopedia of Philosophy, Vol. Summer 2020 ed.
Available online: https://plato.stanford.edu/archives/sum2020/entries/
augustine/.

Turner, Denys (1995). *The Darkness of God: Negativity in Christian
Mysticism*. Cambridge: Cambridge University Press.

Vesty, Lauren (2016). "Millennials Want Purpose over Paychecks. So
Why Can't We Find It at Work?" *The Guardian*, September 14, 2016,
sec. Guardian Sustainable Business. Available online: https://www
.theguardian.com/sustainable-business/2016/sep/14/millennials-work
-purpose-linkedin-survey.

Weber, Max (2001). *The Protestant Ethic and the Spirit of Capitalism*
(Routledge Classics). New York: Routledge.

Weeks, Kathi (2011). *The Problem with Work: Feminism, Marxism,
Antiwork Politics, and Postwork Imaginaries*. Durham: Duke
University Press Books.

Weil, David (2017). *The Fissured Workplace: Why Work Became So
Bad for So Many and What Can Be Done to Improve It*. Reprint ed.
Cambridge; London: Harvard University Press.

Wells, Samuel, Wesley Vander Lugt, and Benjamin Wayman (2018).
Improvisation: The Drama of Christian Ethics. Repackaged ed. Grand
Rapids: Baker Academic.

Wetzel, James (2008). *Augustine and the Limits of Virtue*. 2nd ed.
Cambridge: Cambridge University Press.

Williams, Rowan (2016a). "A Question to Myself: Time and Self-
Awareness in the Confessions." In *On Augustine*, 1–24. New York:
Bloomsbury Continuum.

Williams, Rowan (2016b). "'Good for Nothing'? Augustine on Creation."
In *On Augustine*, 59–78. New York: Bloomsbury Continuum.

Williams, Rowan (2016c). "Good for Nothing? Augustine on Creation."
In *On Augustine*. London; Oxford; New York; New Delhi; Sydney:
Bloomsbury Continuum.

Williams, Rowan (2016d). "Language, Reality and Desire: The Nature
of Christian Formation." In *On Augustine*, 41–58. New York:
Bloomsbury Continuum.

Williams, Rowan (2016e). "Politics and the Soul: Reading the City of
God." In *On Augustine*, 107–30. New York: Bloomsbury Continuum.

Williams, Rowan (2016f). "Sapientia: Wisdom and the Trinitarian Relations."
In *On Augustine*, 171–90. New York: Bloomsbury Continuum.

Wolff, Richard D. (2012). *Democracy at Work: A Cure for Capitalism*.
Chicago: Haymarket Books.

INDEX